The
Common
Market

Also by the author

THE ARABS

The House of Europe, where the European Parliament and the Council of Europe mee

The Common Market

by

HARRY B. ELLIS

THE WORLD PUBLISHING COMPANY

CLEVELAND AND NEW YORK

Published by The World Publishing Company
2231 West 110th Street, Cleveland 2, Ohio
Published simultaneously in Canada by
Nelson, Foster & Scott Ltd.
Library of Congress Catalog Card Number: 65-13078
FIRST EDITION
MWP
Designed by Jack Jaget

To

XENIA

and

FRANK MICHELSON

Some abbreviations of agencies mentioned in the book

CMEA (Comecon)	Council for Mutual Economic Assistance
ECSC	European Coal and Steel Community
EDC	European Defense Community
EEC (Common Market)	European Economic Community
EFTA	European Free Trade Association
EPC	European Political Community
EURATOM	European Atomic Energy Community
GATT	General Agreement on Tariffs and Trade
IBRD	International Bank for Reconstruction and Development (World Bank)
IMF	International Monetary Fund
NATO	North Atlantic Treaty Organization
OECD	Organization for Economic Cooperation and Development
OEEC	Organization for European Economic Cooperation
WEU	Western European Union

Contents

Hills Where Nothing Grows   11

A Thousand Years of Struggle   17

First Steps Toward Unity   27

Coal, Steel, and Jean Monnet   38

The Common Market Itself   58

Farmers and the Common Market   90

Euratom and the "Wise Men"   109

De Gaulle and Nationalism   122

Britain and the Veto   137

The United States and Europe   156

The Iron Curtain Cracks   172

Where Will the Future Lead?   180

Index   199

Hills Where Nothing Grows

Every year on February 21 groups of elderly Frenchmen with military decorations on their blue serge or gray suits march haphazardly toward war memorials in towns and villages throughout France. Many of these men are of the working class, looking somewhat stiff in their unaccustomed Sunday best. Hurrying younger Frenchmen may pause, sobered for an instant, to hear what is being said.

An oldster clears his throat and begins to talk, standing beneath the tricolor flag of France. Among his audience tears glisten on tough old faces that seldom show emotion. These men form a fraternity, dwindling in number year by year, of soldiers who many years ago endured and survived the Battle of Verdun, the longest and most bitterly fought battle of World War I.

For the moment, as they listen, these men have forgotten their cafés, their gardens tended in quiet corners behind old stone walls, their beloved games of bowling played in village squares. They are lost for the moment in the remembrance of another world—the mud, fog, and terror of the trenches of Verdun, where so many of their comrades fell.

On January 22, 1963, forty-seven years after Verdun, two famous men put their names to a treaty signed in Paris. They were President Charles de Gaulle of France and Chancellor Konrad Adenauer of West Germany, and the document they signed was a Treaty of Cooperation, designed to end centuries of enmity between the two neighboring countries along the Rhine. Charles de Gaulle in particular had tasted the bitter fruits of that enmity. As a young French Army captain, he had been wounded and captured by German troops in the Battle of Verdun.

Now the two elder statesmen, de Gaulle in his seventies, Adenauer even older, put their signature to a treaty which each regarded as a climax of his long career. Their signing done, the two proud old men rose and embraced each other with emotion.

Chancellor Konrad Adenauer and President Charles de Gaulle sign the Treaty of Cooperation. French Premier Georges Pompidou, right, is one of the witnesses.

Like most other parts of northeastern France the landscape of Lorraine is peaceful, rising from gently rolling fields on its western side to densely wooded hills in the east. At the southern end of one of these forests, the Argonne, lies the city of Verdun.

To the casual eye Lorraine seems to have slumbered along unchanged through the centuries. Long low farmhouses of stone dot the countryside, their red tile roofs stained green with moss. Villages cluster around their church steeples on the banks of the River Meuse. Early in the evening the farmers of Lorraine draw shut their heavy wooden gates, closing in their courtyards about them. In the towns the housewives lean out windows to shutter up their houses, leaving blank walls to front the narrow streets. Occasionally a café casts a yellow glow across a cobblestoned road. Otherwise the towns lie dark and still throughout the night.

In fact there are stirrings of change beneath this placid surface of Lorraine. In many farms it is now the iron treads of tractors, and not horses' hoofs, that churn the ground into mud and send the chickens flying. As a consequence, the sons of village blacksmiths have moved away or gone into other work, perhaps at the gleaming service stations that have arisen on the outskirts of towns. Here and there shopkeepers have modernized their little stores, though in each shop the wife of the owner still sits watchfully at the cash box near the door.

There is little in these changes, or in the lazy countryside itself, to warn the traveler of what he will find at the city of Verdun. A first hint comes twenty miles west of that city, on the road from Paris, where the ordinary roadside mileage markers disappear, replaced by tall cones of beige concrete, each cone crowned by a ring of stars at the top, with the outline of a lighted torch among the stars. "Voie de la Liberté 1944" —Route of Liberty 1944—is inscribed in blue letters on each cone. Along this road Allied troops in World War II threw back the Germans who had occupied France since 1940.

The cemetery at Verdun

The final approach to the city lies through rougher countryside, wearing a burr of tough grasses and scrub bushes. This is
the Argonne. Its villages seem dark, the houses somber in
gray-black stone. Then comes Verdun itself, today a bustling
manufacturing city of 28,000 persons, sharing in the prosperity
of France.

But the real story of Verdun had unfolded a generation
earlier. Stretching along the narrow upper streets of Verdun
are many older houses, whose walls, during World War I,
echoed daily to the crashing of German guns outside the town.

East of Verdun, crowning the ridges on the other side of the
Meuse, stood a line of forts that became the center of the most
dreadful battle of World War I, possibly in all human history;
a ten-month carnage of massed artillery and infantry charges,
in which more than one million French and German soldiers
were killed, gassed, or wounded. An exact casualty count

could not be made. Even today the bones of fallen men, whether French or German no one can say, still work their way to the surface of the tortured ground. Nine French villages vanished beneath the endless shelling and never were rebuilt. In some places the topsoil was completely blasted away so that almost nothing grows except coarse shrubs and fir trees.

Nearly three-quarters of the French Army poured into the inferno of Verdun during the ten months the battle raged, from February 21, 1916, to the end of that year. "They shall not pass" became the rallying cry of the heroic French defenders. The city held and the Germans did not pass. But a new chapter of aching bitterness had reached out and touched thousands of families on both sides of the Rhine.

To understand the Common Market today, in all its profound importance, the observer must reflect on things quite apart from economics — on those dwindling bands of marching Frenchmen; on that treaty signed in Paris by Adenauer and de Gaulle; and on the dreadful secret concealed by the peaceful landscape of Lorraine, where bulldozers carving out new roads still uncover rusted helmets, both French and German, worn by soldiers fifty years ago.

But why should one understand the Common Market? What is it, and what relationship does it bear to the historical events we have just described? First, the Common Market is an economic association, born in 1958, of six European countries — France, West Germany, Italy, Belgium, Holland, and Luxembourg. Rapidly these six countries are merging their economies into one vast trading unit, within which people, goods, and money will be able to move as freely as Americans cross the borders of their various states.

This means that a French housewife can go to the shelves of her grocer and select competitively among fruits, cookies, cheeses, and canned vegetables produced in six countries instead of one. She and her husband can go to a department store in Paris and choose among refrigerators made in France, West Germany, and Italy—all being offered in Paris at about the same price.

This association called the Common Market means better goods at lower prices, which in turn leads to expanded production, more jobs, and greater prosperity in Europe. This is beneficial, but does not in itself explain why the Common Market is essential for us to understand. The real meaning of the Common Market lies deeper.

Wise leaders in Europe, after the bitterness of World War II, foresaw a merging of the economic interests of their peoples as the best hope of burying forever the old national rivalries which had involved Europe, time and again, in war. Let us unify our economies, the leaders reasoned, and what once had been national interests will become common interests, to be protected and nurtured by all. No longer would the great beds of coal and iron underlying France, Germany, and Belgium be a source of rivalry and tug of war, but a sinew of strength to be shared. As the basic means of production became commonly controlled, the threat of war progressively would disappear. Far down the road glimmered an even bolder hope—an eventual United States of Europe, growing from the Common Market.

Already this young association of six countries has become the second largest trading unit in the world, after the United States of America. Young nations of Africa, old nations of the Middle East, other countries of Europe, the United States itself—all are striving to adjust themselves to this potent new force in the trading world.

To uncover the roots of this historic development, to trace its meaning for today and for the future, we must travel back through the history of Europe, more than a thousand years.

A Thousand Years of Struggle

One day in the year 843 A.D. three brothers met in the town of Verdun to divide an inheritance from their grandfather. These brothers, named Charles the Bald, Louis the German, and Lothair, were grandsons of the man who might be called the first real European—Charlemagne, or Charles the Great, Emperor of the Franks. No man before Charlemagne had united Europe nor has any man since in a lasting rule, though many, like Napoleon and Hitler, have dreamed of so doing. To Charlemagne alone belongs the distinction of having welded western and central Europe into a single empire.

So vast was this empire of Charlemagne that a soldier of his host, marching on foot across the lands of his royal master, would have taken two months to complete the journey. France, Germany, Belgium, Holland, Luxembourg, Switzerland, Italy, and parts of Spain, Poland, Czechoslovakia, Austria, Hungary, and Yugoslavia—all these countries, as they are named today, fell to Charlemagne, during his fifty-three military campaigns and nearly fifty years of rule.

Great as he was, Charlemagne had not built from scratch. His father, Pepin the Short, and Pepin's father, Charles Martel (Charles the Hammer), had done the first rugged work of

Charlemagne. The ruler welded western and central Europe into a single empire.

empire building. In 732 the Arabs, already the conquerors of the Middle East, North Africa, and Spain, had surged up into France, or Gaul as it then was known.

Near Tours the charge of the Arab cavalry, flying the green banner of the Prophet Mohammed, was shattered by the mail-clad troops of Charles Martel. Three years later the Hammer repeated the lesson, driving the Arabs from Arles and Avignon in southwestern Gaul.

Partly for this service to Christian Europe, the Roman Catholic Pope legalized the Carolingian dynasty by anointing Pepin the Short, son of the Hammer, as king of the Franks, replacing the Merovingian dynasty which had gone before. Pope Stephen, moreover, crossing the Alps from Italy into

France to bless Pepin, ordered the Franks to choose their future kings from the Carolingian house alone.

His way thus smoothed to conquer all Gaul, King Pepin added much of Germany to the kingdom he left to his eldest son, Charlemagne. It was on these foundations that Charlemagne built the empire of the Franks.

The lasting significance of Charlemagne's work was not territorial, for the empire itself split up soon after his death. But Charlemagne, through his conquests, had enlarged the borders of Christian Europe and then sealed them off against alien attacks launched by Moslems from Spain and by Avars (descendants of the Huns) and by wild Germanic tribes from the east. Thus protected, the missionaries of Rome carried Latin Christianity throughout the forests of Germany and gave to Europe its first sense of a common faith and culture.

Behind the ramparts of empire trade flourished and new lands were broken to the plow. Great abbeys sprang up, around which townships gathered. Learning spread and monks clad in robes and sandals, working in dismal cells, hand-lettered manuscripts whose luminous pages of gold, silver, scarlet, and blue still glow in museums throughout Europe.

Charlemagne himself died in 814, but the grand lines of his policy persisted over centuries, long after his empire had dissolved into warring factions. Latin Europe, though divided within itself, remained an entity distinct not only from Islamic Spain but from the eastern Europe of the Slavs. Down through the ages after Charlemagne Frenchmen, Germans, Belgians, and Dutchmen never wholly lost a flickering sense of kinship, even as they fought.

A fatal flaw in the Frankish social system was the division of a family's inheritance, whether farm or empire, among the sons, so that centralized control over property was lost. This flaw had splintered the Merovingian kingdom, also Frankish,

Lothair. This image is from the Lothair Cross in the Cathedral at Aachen.

which had preceded Charles Martel. Now it was to crumble Charlemagne's legacy as well.

Charles the Bald, Louis the German, and Lothair, meeting at Verdun to parcel out their grandfather's empire, were enemies as well as brothers. In an oath taken at the city of Strasbourg on the Rhine River, Charles and Louis had sworn an alliance against their brother, Lothair. In such a mood of suspicion, eying each other jealously, the three men divided Europe. Charles the Bald received the western part of the empire, or roughly what is France today. Louis the German took the eastern portion, corresponding to Germany. To Lothair fell a long broad strip in between, extending from the North Sea down through Europe into Italy. To his kingdom Lothair gave the name Lotharingia, the origin of the modern word Lorraine.

Unlike the kingdoms of Charles and Louis, Lotharingia had no semblance of unity. It was a heterogeneous mixture of peoples, an indeterminate buffer zone between France and

Germany. Of all the enmities that have ravaged Europe, none has been more persistent than that between Frenchmen and Germans, and over the centuries this rivalry has centered on Alsace and Lorraine, the territories of Lothair.

The very name "France" connotes something German. For the first few centuries after Christ, when Gaul was ruled by Rome, the land was inhabited by a mingling of ancient stocks, mainly Celtic, making up a people called Gauls.

In the fifth century A.D. Gaul began to be penetrated by Germanic tribes, themselves driven westward by the invasion of central Europe by Mongolian Huns. Gradually this flood of Germanic tribes—Visigoths, Burgundians, Franks, and others—inundated the land of Gaul and made it their own.

Of these tribes the Franks proved dominant and to the nation that gradually developed they gave their name. In the days of Charlemagne, Germany was called East Francia, or eastern France. The peoples of the empire, mostly of Teutonic (German) stock, had no notion of themselves as "Frenchmen" or "Germans." This distinction was to come later and the Partition of Verdun, engineered by Charles, Louis, and Lothair, helped to breed it.

Under Charles the Fat, third son of Louis the German, there was a brief paper restoration of the empire. But this was transitory and the process of dissolution went on, with Lotharingia in particular separating into petty principalities and fiefs. During the Middle Ages these central territories belonged mainly to Germany, grouped within the Holy Roman Empire.

In 1552 the Kingdom of France occupied the three Bishoprics of Metz, Toul, and Verdun, taking these parts of former Lotharingia away from German control for the first time since the Partition of Verdun. In 1648, at the end of a long European war, France consolidated this gain by obtaining full sovereignty over Alsace, hereditary to the French crown. This apparent enrichment, greeted with joy in Paris, was in fact a darkling day for France.

In 1681 King Louis XIV of France deepened the humiliation of Germany by fortifying Strasbourg, capital of Alsace, and extending French holdings throughout Alsace and Lorraine. Rough conduct by French soldiers during these latter campaigns of the Sun King hardened German opinion against French control along the Rhine.

But Germany's day of revenge was still far off. Deliberately kept decentralized and hence militarily weak by German noblemen, each jealous of his own preserve, the German portions of the Holy Roman Empire proved unable to counter effectively a unified France. In 1738 all of Lorraine, the prize of shrewd French diplomacy and a short war, followed Alsace into the hereditary possession of the kings of France.

Later in the eighteenth century the rulers of France, absorbed by their perennial quarrel with Austria, seat of the Holy Roman Empire, allied themselves with a rude Protestant power, new on the European scene. This power was Prussia, formerly a northeastern German province of the Holy Roman Empire, but now a thrusting young kingdom, led by the House of Hohenzollern, a disciplined family with ambitions of its own.

As Sparta had been in ancient Greece, so Prussia had become in Europe by 1750—a symbol of militarism, its tough soldiers respected throughout the Continent, though the land that had bred those troops was small and poor by comparison with the imperial powers that surrounded it. Although temporarily allied with France, the House of Hohenzollern had its eyes fixed on eventual control of all Germany, which inevitably would bring it into conflict with France along the Rhine.

The next heroic figure to step onto the stage of this Franco-German rivalry was Napoleon. In 1801 the great Corsican, having defeated the Austrian Empire, advanced the eastern frontier of France uniformly to the Rhine. Beyond this, Napoleon's troops rolled on through Germany.

Suppressing many small German states, creating others, using Germany always as a reservoir of men and money for his major war against England, Napoleon's rule helped to create a sense of German nationalism among peoples who for generations had been politically divided into more than a hundred states. The anvil on which German nationalism was forged was a growing passion to be rid of the French invader.

A leader in this German revival was Prussia. From the German War of Liberation (1813) Prussia emerged as political tutor of a string of buffer states in western Germany, designed to keep France safely behind the Rhine. By 1866, under the brilliant but ruthless leadership of Otto von Bismarck, Prussia had ejected the rival influence of Austria and had become the virtual master of Germany.

Bismarck's next object was to work toward war with France, with the aim of extending German power west of the Rhine and depriving the traditional enemy of a natural frontier. Fruition of Bismarck's plans came in the war of 1870–1871, during which the French Army was defeated and Prussian guns bombarded Paris. An exultant Germany entered into sovereign control over Alsace and much of Lorraine.

The pendulum had now swung back. These provinces, which had been nominally German in the first centuries after the Partition of Verdun and then had become solidly French under the Bourbon kings and Napoleon, once again were German—though the farmers, herdsmen, and townspeople who inhabited the fields and forests of Alsace-Lorraine had had little or no voice in these myriad changes.

With Prussian thoroughness the conqueror strove to Germanize his new border lands. Visually he would seem to have succeeded. Even today a visitor to Strasbourg might think he was in Germany. Houses with overhanging wooden balconies, decked with flowers, rise sharply to pointed roofs. The people who live in these houses are broad-faced and thick-bodied, unlike the quick gesticulating type one thinks of as French. Alsatian restaurants feature sauerkraut, garnished with sausages and pork chops. Huge men with rolls of fat at the back of their necks drink Alsatian beer beneath German poetry on the walls.

An old street in Strasbourg, city of the House of Europe

Above all it is the language of Strasbourg that strikes the ear as German—a guttural dialect, basically German, with French words mixed in. A Frenchman from Paris, stopping at a Strasbourg hotel, might be unable to understand his chambermaid, though by citizenship and in her heart she is as French as he. Yet a German visitor from across the Rhine could talk easily with the girl.

No sooner had Strasbourg fallen to the enemy in 1871 than the people of Paris showed their loyalty to the lost provinces. Each day they brought flowers to the feet of the huge statue of a woman, representing the city of Strasbourg, which stands in the Place de la Concorde in Paris, looking out across the square where the guillotine once stood. For more than forty years the people of Paris garlanded their statue in this way, as a sign of their determination to regain Alsace-Lorraine. "Speak of it never, think of it always," advised the French statesman Léon Gambetta, during the long years when eastern France was German.

Deliverance came at the end of World War I, following that fearful trench warfare, epitomized by the Battle of Verdun. From 1919 to 1940 Alsace-Lorraine remained French. Then Adolf Hitler provided the next turn of the wheel. His gray-clad soldiers swept through the conquest of France; Paris itself was occupied by the Germans, and Alsace-Lorraine, rich in coal and iron as well as tradition, belonged again to Germany.

Hitler was determined that Alsace in particular should bear the German stamp forever. No word of French was allowed to be spoken, written, or read throughout the province. Shopkeepers were forced to take down their French signs and replace them with German. Mail boxes, fire alarms, and road signs changed their nationality. Streets were renamed, though in at least one instance a local German official made an innocent or shrewd mistake; the "Street of the Savage" in Mulhouse became "Adolf Hitler Street"!

The German surrender at the end of World War II brought back the eastern provinces to France. But this time victory was different. Terrible though the trench warfare of World War I had been, its battles had been fought out primarily between soldiers. Civilian populations had escaped relatively unscathed. Not so during the second war. Cities had fallen in ruins beneath the weight of German and Allied bombs. Factories had been smashed, people were hungry, victors and vanquished alike.

The peoples of Europe emerged from this war indescribably weary, profoundly disillusioned with the political and economic conditions that had bred the holocaust. Their Europe, like a richly colored pageant down through the ages, had produced a splendid civilization, beautifully symbolized by the Gothic cathedrals of France, embracing within their soaring walls marvels of painting, sculpture, stained glass, and architecture.

But this same Europe, by breeding nationalism, division, and hence revenge, had nearly destroyed itself. One of these historic struggles we have traced—the rivalry between Frenchmen and Germans for the lands along the Rhine. But there had been other ancient quarrels—between Slavs and Germans, between English and French, and, on a wider scale, between Catholics and Protestants, the heirs of Rome and the disciples of Calvin and Luther.

Clearly this old Europe of rampant nationalism had led to a dead end, overpowered by the scope of modern weaponry. At the heart of postwar Europe lay the six countries which later would form the Common Market. Every one of them had been overrun by alien armies during World War II. Wise leaders among them, Frenchmen, Germans, Belgians, and others—backed up by the weariness of their peoples—perceived that Europe must start down a bold new road, away from the ruins of the past.

First Steps Toward Unity

Clearly the new road must lead toward some form of international co-operation, to prevent a recurrence of nationalistic disaster. A startling initiative had been taken at the very beginning of World War II when Winston Churchill, Prime Minister of Britain, proposed that England and France merge into a single nation-state, with joint citizenship for their peoples. Made in the first hurried hours of war, this dramatic proposal was forgotten in the rush of events, including the fall of France to the Nazis.

But again it was Winston Churchill, speaking at the University of Zurich on September 19, 1946, who rallied postwar Europe toward the concept of unity, by demanding "an act of faith in the European family," culminating in a "kind of United States of Europe." Already a crop of so-called European movements was sprouting in England and on the Continent, grouping unity-minded organizations in France, Germany, Italy, Belgium, Holland, and Greece. In part these strivings toward unity drew their inspiration from efforts launched before World War II by men such as Aristide Briand of France and Count Richard N. Coudenhove-Kalergi of Hungary.

27

Paul Henri Spaak of Belgium

Two distinct trends emerged in these early postwar gropings toward European unity. One group of men aimed at the elimination of all national barriers, with the hope of creating a huge integrated market whose economic progress would be unimpeded by frontier obstructions like tariffs, customs, and quotas. Advocates of this school of thought, led by Jean Monnet of France, Paul Henri Spaak of Belgium, and others, held that only through a wide sharing of economic benefits among all classes, within a democratic framework, could communism be prevented from thrusting into the void of postwar Europe.

The second trend was conservative and Roman Catholic,

aspiring to a cluster of Catholic states—France, West Germany, Italy, possibly Spain and Portugal—which would form a Christian bastion against communism and, in the thoughts of some, against socialism as well. General de Gaulle, leader of Free France during the war, at first had conceived of European unity in terms of a combination of France, Italy, Portugal, and Spain. Others who shared this general Catholic orientation were Alcide de Gasperi of Italy and the West German leader, Konrad Adenauer.

Throughout the succeeding development of the European unity movement, these two threads of policy remained strangely mixed. In the Common Market today only Holland of the six member states is predominantly Protestant. Yet the economic rules governing the operation of the European Economic Community (Common Market) were largely developed and administered by "technocrats," often Socialist-minded and in some cases Protestant.

In December 1947 these various European movements converged in the International Committee of the Movements for European Unity, charged with organizing a Congress of Europe to be held in The Hague, capital of the Netherlands. At this congress, convened from May 7–10, 1948, "Europe" was institutionalized for the first time. With the goal of promoting political and economic unity on the Continent, the Hague Congress initiated a Council of Europe to include a Consultative Assembly (Parliament), a Committee of Ministers, and a permanent secretariat. Strasbourg, capital of Alsace, was chosen as the home of the new organization and in 1950 a special "House of Europe" was constructed for it. Alsace, heartland of the ancient Franco-German rivalry, was to become, symbolically at least, a hub of the brave new Europe.

This Council of Europe, starting with ten members, came

formally into being on May 5, 1949. Today the council has a membership of seventeen nations.[1]

As a forum for airing European questions, the Council of Europe does much useful work. One of its most far-reaching accomplishments was the creation of a European Convention on Human Rights, designed to safeguard the fundamental rights and freedoms of citizens of member states, backed up by the enforcement machinery of a European Commission on Human Rights and a European Court. One of these rights, "freedom from torture," might sound strange to Americans. Yet recent European history includes several examples of torture being used as an instrument of policy, as by the Nazis in Germany and by elements of the French Army in Algeria. Europeans were keenly aware that protection from torture, along with freedom of worship and other rights, was an essential element of their armor of human dignity.

Sixteen member states of the Council of Europe have signed the human rights convention and nine so far have accepted the jurisdiction of the European Court as binding.[2] This means that a citizen of one of these countries, aggrieved by what he considers an unjust action taken against him by his own government, can appeal for redress through machinery set up

[1] Austria, Belgium, Cyprus, Denmark, France, the Federal Republic of Germany, Greece, Iceland, the Republic of Ireland, Italy, Luxembourg, the Netherlands, Norway, Sweden, Switzerland, Turkey, and the United Kingdom (Britain). Israel has observer status in the Consultative Assembly, and Spain and the Vatican are members of the Council for Cultural Cooperation, a subsidiary body of the Council of Europe.

[2] Switzerland has not signed the human rights convention. A problem is that Swiss women do not have the right to vote. The human rights convention provides for free elections, secret ballots, and other guarantees of democracy. Separately the convention stipulates that all rights guaranteed by the convention shall apply equally to men and women. Apparently Switzerland must change its law to sign the human rights convention, or sign with reservations.

by the Council of Europe. If the European Court finds his complaint justified, the offending government must bow to the international decision and satisfy its citizen.

Since it entered into force on September 3, 1953, the European Convention on Human Rights has caused one member nation to alter its Constitution; three others have made changes in their internal laws, and international bodies in Asia, Africa, and the Americas have called for similar "supreme courts" on their continents.

Illustrative of the earnest "European" approach of the Council of Europe is its seating arrangement in the Consultative Assembly. Deputies chosen by their seventeen national parliaments sit alphabetically in the House of Europe in Strasbourg. Thus, through the accident of names, a Conservative Party delegate from Britain may sit next to a Socialist from Italy, who in turn may be flanked by a deputy from Greece. Few if any other parliaments in the world can match this salt-and-pepper mixture, designed to achieve a truly international outlook.

Periodically the Strasbourg assembly still rings to the expression of inspired oratory. Yet the structure of the Council of Europe contained a weakness which destined this organization to be elbowed out of the mainstream of the European unity movement. Its Consultative Assembly, devoid of real power, can only submit resolutions to the Committee of Ministers. This latter body, rather than act by itself, recommends decisions to the member governments it represents. Real power continued to reside in national governments which, except in limited fields such as human rights, yielded no sovereignty to the Council of Europe.

We turn now to the military aspect of European integration. Immediately after the war Allied attention was focused on preventing a renewal of German aggression and to this end

Britain and France in 1947 signed a mutual defense pact, called the Dunkirk Treaty. But swiftly Western leaders, urged on by the warning voice of Winston Churchill, came to realize that the real threat of the future lay in the enormous weight of Communist Russia, already consolidating its iron grip on Eastern Europe and thrusting ponderously toward the West.

In February 1948 the Communist coup d'état in Prague added Czechoslovakia to the long list of satellites—including Poland, Hungary, Romania, Bulgaria, Yugoslavia, and the eastern zone of Germany—already under the Soviet yoke. In April of that year Moscow added to the pressure by clamping a land blockade on occupied Berlin, in an effort to force the United States, Britain, and France out of the divided city. The blockade failed only through a massive months-long airlift mounted by the United States and Britain, during which almost every necessity of food and fuel was flown in to the beleaguered people of Berlin.

Reacting to the Soviet menace, five European powers— Britain, France, Belgium, the Netherlands, and Luxembourg —signed in March 1948 the Brussels Treaty, pledging the signatories to mutual defense in the event of military attack. Clearly, however, the nations of Western Europe, just beginning to recover from the exhaustion of World War II, could not face the Soviet Union alone. Only the United States could provide the needed balance of power.

On April 4, 1949, representatives of the United States, Canada, and ten European nations signed in Washington the North Atlantic Treaty, which for the first time since 1800 committed the United States to the defense of Europe in time of peace. Article 5 of the treaty bound the contracting parties to regard "an armed attack against one or more of them in Europe or North America" as an attack against them all.

To give force to this declaration the twelve members, later

expanded to fifteen,[3] established a unified defense command outside Paris, to which each government pledged to contribute troops. The United States for its part initially furnished four divisions of soldiers and one billion dollars to finance the first year's operations of the North Atlantic Treaty Organization (NATO). Named as the first Supreme Commander, Allied Powers, Europe, was General Dwight D. Eisenhower, who had become the symbol of Allied unity during World War II.

Here was truly a revolution in American policy. For more than 150 years the United States had faithfully followed George Washington's counsel "to steer clear of permanent alliances with any part of the foreign world." Not since the abrogation of a treaty of alliance with France in 1800 had the United States bound itself to defend another power. Twice this isolation had been broken, in 1917 and 1941, when American soldiers had gone to Europe to help defeat Germany.

The second of these world wars had stimulated a profound change in American thinking. Clearly postwar Europe constituted a vacuum into which the Soviet Union might have rushed. This would have faced the United States with an enemy potentially more powerful than itself, an enemy possessed of the entire continent of Europe and stretching eastward across Asia to the Pacific. The only way to prevent this calamity was to commit the United States to the defense of Europe, before the Soviets could move.

In another sense NATO spelled a revolution. Germany, the historic aggressor in Europe, whose armies twice in this century had struck terror across the Continent, was welcomed

[3] Belgium, Canada, Denmark, the Federal Republic of Germany (West Germany), France, Greece, Iceland, Italy, Luxembourg, the Netherlands, Norway, Portugal, Turkey, the United Kingdom, and the United States.

into the alliance as a full-fledged partner. Behind this act of apparent magnanimity lay the realization that West Germany, if rejected from the Western community, would be forced to act strictly on its own, or might gravitate toward the East.

How much better to include West Germany in a Western partnership, with the aim of making her future interests coincide with those of the Allied community the Germans so often had fought. To give the German people a sense of responsibility and "belonging" seemed the safest way to prevent a resurgence of dangerous German nationalism. The revulsion of the German people against the destructive effects of Hitler's war made the moment ripe.

But partnership implied a genuine share in Western defense, particularly since West Germany, fronting on the Iron Curtain, would bear the brunt of any Soviet aggression. This meant guns in German hands and a new German Army, an eventuality dreaded by many Europeans. An important step was taken in 1954, when the West German Government voluntarily gave up the right to manufacture atomic, biological, and chemical weapons (the so-called ABC weapons). This paved the way for West Germany's entry into NATO on May 9, 1955, and unanimous agreement that the new partner should raise twelve divisions for the NATO command. This obligation has been fulfilled and West Germany today is the strongest conventional military power in NATO, after the United States.

Eventually a purely military partnership would have sunk of its own weight, if unaccompanied by European economic recovery. This recovery was far from being achieved at the time Allied planners signed the NATO treaty in Washington. The cold winds of an unusually hard winter in 1946–1947 had blown through the cracks of European economic weakness and had shown how unable the Continent was to cope with its enormous tasks of reconstruction. On June 5, 1947, in an address at Harvard University, Secretary of State George C. Marshall offered a helping hand to Europe that was as revolutionary, in its way, as the later North Atlantic Treaty was to be.

Painting "the dislocation of the entire fabric of European economy," General Marshall declared that "Europe's requirements for the next three or four years of foreign food and other essential products—principally from America—are so much greater than her present ability to pay that she must have substantial additional help or face economic, social, and political deterioration of a very grave character . . .

"It is logical," the secretary of state continued, "that the United States should do whatever it is able to do to assist in the return of normal economic health in the world, without which there can be no political stability and no assured peace."

This made sense for the United States itself. Dollar-short Europe was running a huge annual deficit in its balance of payments with the United States, meaning that European countries simply could not pay for the goods they needed to buy. It was not up to the United States to legislate a program of European recovery. This must be done by the Europeans themselves. They must join hands to plan their own recovery and to administer it. Then the United States would foot the bill—not as a give-away program, but to restore a healthy economic balance in the world, so that, among other things, American traders would have future markets in which to sell.

General Marshall's proposal fell upon Europe as an electrifying call. Sixteen, and later eighteen, European governments banded together in the Organization for European Economic Cooperation. Founded on April 16, 1948, the OEEC presented to the United States a coherent plan for Europe's economic recovery. (General Marshall's original proposal had been open to all European governments, including Communist. But the Soviet Union kept aloof and forbade its satellites to join. Thus the OEEC was confined to free world nations. In 1960, when the balance of payments was running the other way and the United States itself needed help, the OEEC was expanded to include the United States and Canada and was renamed the Organization for Economic Cooperation and Development, or OECD.[4])

On the American side, the United States Congress in April 1948 created the Economic Cooperation Administration, through which would be channeled a four-year program of American economic assistance to Europe. Seventeen billion dollars was appropriated for the purpose. The subsequent success of this Marshall Plan allowed the program to be terminated nine months ahead of schedule, at a cost of four and a half billion dollars less than originally had been planned.

By 1950, five years after the end of the war, the free world had come a long way from the chaos which had prevailed in Europe when the guns fell silent. On the military side there was NATO, weak-muscled compared to its later strength, but none the less a trans-Atlantic partnership for mutual defense. Also stretching across the Atlantic was the Marshall Plan, with its European counterpart of the OEEC. Other international organizations had been formed to aid the process of recovery, including the International Monetary Fund (IMF), the International Bank for Reconstruction and Development (IBRD, or World Bank), and the General Agreement on Tariffs and Trade (GATT). And among the Europeans them-

[4] Members of the OECD are Austria, Belgium, Canada, Denmark, France, the Federal Republic of Germany, Greece, Iceland, the Republic of Ireland, Italy, Luxembourg, the Netherlands, Norway, Portugal, Spain, Sweden, Switzerland, Turkey, the United Kingdom, and the United States.

selves stood the Council of Europe, a romantic though largely powerless expression of striving toward integration.

But all these undertakings, however valuable in themselves, represented *co-operation* among sovereign states. They did not extend to *unity*, which implied the cession of at least some national sovereignty to a supranational, or centralized, body. A modest start toward unity had been made by Belgium, the Netherlands, and Luxembourg, when in 1948 they had established a Benelux customs union among them. But essentially the great step, which would lead from co-operation to real unity in Europe, remained to be taken.

Coal, Steel, and Jean Monnet

When history has gained its perspective on our age, two men are likely to emerge as the towering Frenchmen of their times. One is Charles de Gaulle, the President of France. The other is Jean Monnet, who more than any other man has been the moving force and inspiration behind the European unity movement. Physically, de Gaulle is tall, aloof, and commanding; Monnet is short, friendly, mild in appearance. But even greater than this physical disparity is their divergence of outlook. General de Gaulle has put all the force of his tremendous talent to work for the grandeur of France. Jean Monnet has looked beyond national goals to the union of Europe and, beyond that, to an Atlantic partnership between Europe and the United States.

Born in the French town of Cognac in 1888, Monnet at the age of thirty-one became Deputy Secretary General of the League of Nations, presaging his later international career. As an international banker between the two world wars, he came to know businessmen, economists, and government officials in many countries, including the United States, where for a time Mr. Monnet was a member of a Wall Street investment firm. In Europe, he helped stabilize the currencies of Poland, Austria, and Romania. Three years of his career Monnet spent in China, advising the government on the reorganization of its railroads. All this was grist for his mill, when later he would turn his attention to the problems of a war-shattered Europe.

Today Monnet seems like a friendly grandfather, but one extremely wise, to whom one listens with respect. Once in Paris he and I rode up together in a tiny French elevator, like a birdcage for two. Only seconds before we had met for the first time. Yet by the time the elevator had reached our floor, we were chatting warmly.

During the luncheon that followed I watched this extraordinary man, then in his mid-seventies. He drank no wine and ate sparingly. When the waiter offered him brandy after the meal, he declined, until the waiter pressed the dusty bottle before his gaze. It was a cognac made by the Monnet family concern, where Monnet had started his business career. Smiling, he accepted a sip.

During this luncheon he spoke of his experience with the Chinese. "I never knew what they were thinking," I remember him saying. "They were wiser and more subtle than I. But we had business to accomplish. So I made absolutely sure they knew what I was thinking, that they knew just where I stood. That way I gained their confidence and things went along."

This is a hallmark of Monnet—original ideas, expressed clearly, simply, with no equivocation, repeated as often as needed, until they are accepted as part of the currency of other men's thinking.

We have spoken of Churchill's dramatic proposal of 1940 that France and England should become one country. In fact it was Jean Monnet, then working in London to co-ordinate Allied military procurement, who had drafted the idea and persuaded Churchill and de Gaulle to accept it. This is another hallmark of Monnet—to work behind the scenes, an "operator" he has been called, so that often other men's names have been attached to the fruits of his own work.

So it was on May 9, 1950, when French Foreign Minister Robert Schuman, speaking in a glittering salon of the Quai d'Orsay in Paris, declared the French Government's intention "to place the whole of Franco-German coal and steel output under a common High Authority, in an organization open to the participation of the other countries of Europe." In plain words, France and Germany would pool under common ownership the coal and iron ore of the German Ruhr and the French Alsace-Lorraine, which geographically lay side by side, but which had been divided by national frontiers. No longer would there be, as in the past, pulling and hauling between the two nations over the industrial sinews of war and peace. Such a merger, Schuman said, "will make it plain that any war between France and Germany becomes not merely unthinkable but materially impossible." One country no longer could divert to war-making uses the steel which both countries shared.

The words of this stirring initiative were read by Robert Schuman, with Jean Monnet seated modestly at his side, and to this day the plan that resulted in the European Coal and Steel Community is called the Schuman Plan. But the ideas behind the declaration, and the complex work of inter-governmental persuasion, had stemmed primarily from Monnet. Schuman himself, brought up in Lorraine and speaking both French and German, knew by instinct and experience the need for French and German reconciliation. Other European statesmen had played important roles.

But essentially the Schuman Plan bore Monnet's stamp, the result in part of his own postwar work as director of

*Robert Schuman and Jean Monnet, founders of the
European Coal and Steel Community*

French economic recovery. That work had taught him that French recovery had restricted limits, so long as the country's economy was forced to operate within a relatively narrow market. Persistently Monnet drew attention to the example of the United States—one vast integrated market, open equally to manufacturers in California and Massachusetts, with no artificial barriers set up by the states against the movement of goods. Western Europe, by contrast, within an area smaller than that of the United States, was split up into separate national markets, each partially shut off from the others by tariffs, quotas, and other protectionist walls. In a world of giants—the United States and the Soviet Union—Europe was stifling its own growth and its ability to compete by artificial restrictions.

A single open market in Europe, containing 170,000,000 consumers, would encourage mass production, which in turn would lead to lower unit costs, full employment of men and machinery, and broader research on product improvement. A firm with a potentially huge market of buyers would dare to specialize in those goods which it best could produce. Finally, the individual consumer in a giant market, freed of customs duties, tariffs, and quota walls, would be offered a wide range of product choice, impelling manufacturers to keep prices down and quality high.

A shoe manufacturer in Italy, for example, knowing that Italians must wear shoes and that foreign shoes could not enter the Italian market, might have little incentive to make better shoes at lower prices. But if all restrictions were to be swept away, so that foreign shoes could be sold freely in Italian stores, that manufacturer would be forced to compete —or go out of business. This would be good for the consumer and, if repeated broadly enough in many fields, would stimulate the economy of the country as a whole.

None of this, however, could be achieved in postwar Europe without political reconciliation between France and Germany. As Monnet himself put it: "Had the traditional relations between France and Germany been maintained, their desire to dominate each other would have led to new disasters."

There were ample signs that the old suspicions and distrusts had not yet disappeared. Throughout the war General de Gaulle's single-minded goal had been to restore the integrity of France and to this end he had proposed that the industrially rich Ruhr should be taken away from Germany. In 1947 he modified this proposal to a suggestion for international control, under which German coal and steel would be owned by the Allies. In 1949 the International Authority of the Ruhr emerged, giving the United States, Britain, and France ultimate control over much of German industry. This was a harness within which the minority partner—Germany—could not be expected to pull smoothly. Resentments were bound to thicken.

Monnet saw the problem differently. France and Germany must be given a sense of common interests, transcending and submerging the traditional concept of separate national interests. This could only be done by sharing ownership of something vital to both. Where to start? Where better than with coal and steel, the raw stuff of war, in the Ruhr and Alsace-Lorraine, heartland of the historic rivalry? This sharing must be made equal. France, the victor, must throw her resources into the common pool, along with Germany, the vanquished.

"Between countries (France and Germany) that had been divided for so many centuries," Monnet declared, "whose past interests and traditions drew them apart, it was necessary to create a common interest. For some matters, at least, they must find themselves all on the same side of the table, so to speak, solving the same problems from the same standpoint and therefore applying the same rules. To make sure these rules were applied, common institutions had to be created and entrusted with this task."

Chief among these institutions would be an independent High Authority, or management committee, responsible to no single government, but acting as an impartial referee, balancing and safeguarding everyone's interests. This High Authority would be given power to create, within the countries concerned, a common market for coal, steel, iron ore, and scrap by abolishing tariffs, internal subsidies, and other barriers. Ideally this common market should be extended beyond France and Germany, for nature, heedless of the later political divisions of men, also had underlain Belgium, Holland, and Luxembourg with rich veins of iron and coal.

This was the thinking that produced the Schuman Plan; this was the breakthrough, reaching beyond mere co-operation among sovereign states toward the realm of actual unity. Long before Robert Schuman had made his formal declaration of policy, Monnet had been busy with spadework. First he had kindled enthusiasm in Schuman himself, who in turn had sold the idea to the French Government. Outside the borders of France, Monnet and others had found response from Konrad Adenauer, postwar Chancellor of West Germany, from Alcide de Gasperi and Count Carlo Sforza, respectively prime minister and foreign minister of Italy, and from Belgian Socialist leader Paul Henri Spaak.

From the time Schuman stepped before the microphones in the Quai d'Orsay, progress was rapid, considering the courage it took for governments to accept his proposal. Less than a year later, on April 18, 1951, six governments—representing France, West Germany, Italy, Belgium, the Netherlands, and Luxembourg—had signed an agreement in principle. By the next summer all six parliaments had ratified the agreement and the European Coal and Steel Community (ECSC) came into being. Its formal birth date was February 10, 1953, when the High Authority assumed its functions.

Those were heady days in Europe. "This was a human experience of a rare order," an associate of Monnet's told me. "For a vital kernel of people, forging the common institutions, suspicion was replaced by mutual trust in each other, regardless of nationality." The conviction spread among these men that they were allies, working for the common good.

A sense of confidence sprang up that European problems could be solved. France became the first nation to accept German soldiers for training on her soil. At first the soldiers came over quietly at night, in civilian clothes. But soon they were walking, talking, shopping in French towns, dressed in full uniform. I have watched German soldiers, clad in the familiar gray-green cloth of the Wehrmacht, strolling in the streets of Fontainebleau, attracting scarcely a glance from Frenchmen. Yet twenty years before, German soldiers had marched into France as conquerors.

Another problem which the ECSC helped to solve was that of the Saar, a territory rich in coal which after World War II had been taken away from Germany and attached to France. A convention signed in 1949 called the Saar politically auton-omous but economically French, an awkward solution which strained relations between France and Germany. Into this tension like an emollient came the Schuman Plan, concen-trating French and German attention on larger and common interests. In 1956, her war bitterness eased and accustomed to the new partnership, France returned the Saar to Germany.

The pooling of European coal and steel was an end in itself, but it was also a beginning. Schuman had said in his historic declaration of 1950: "Europe will not be made all at once, or according to a single, general plan. It will be built through concrete achievements . . . The pooling of coal and steel pro-duction will immediately provide for the setting-up of com-mon bases for economic development as a first step in the federation of Europe . . ." Years later Monnet wrote of the Coal and Steel Community as having "created a silent revo-lution in men's minds," paving the way for further steps toward unity.

The key to Monnet's thought lay in the concept of *institu-tions*. A treaty without institutions is a piece of paper, which can be torn up. But an institution, set up to perform a con-crete task, manifestly beneficial to all, becomes an entity in itself, accumulating experience and vitality, which a government can destroy only by overriding the interests of all, including its own citizens. Furthermore, a successful institution prepares men's minds to accept new and larger combinations, embracing wider functions.

Institutionally, the ECSC consists of a nine-member High Authority, to which is attached a Consultative Committee; a 142-member European Parliament (originally smaller and called the Common Assembly); a Council of Ministers, where each of the six member governments is directly represented; and a Court of Justice. Headquarters of the High Authority and of the Court of Justice is Luxembourg City; the parliament sits in Strasbourg, using the House of Europe originally built for the Council of Europe.

Decisions of the High Authority, of which Jean Monnet became the first president, have the force of law in the six member countries. This striking fact points up the supranational quality of this executive body of the ECSC. Given wide powers to control the coal and steel industries of the Six, the High Authority's first task was to create a common market in these products by wiping out tariffs, quotas, and all internal restrictions that artificially benefited one member's industry over another's. This task accomplished, the High Authority watched over and guided the operation of the common market it had established, using its Consultative Committee as a point of contact with business, labor, and official groups.

Among the nine members of the High Authority are industrialists, trade unionists, and former government officials, assuring a broad variety of viewpoints on this decision-making body. In a sense each member of the High Authority forgets his nationality. Upon appointment he solemnly swears neither to seek nor accept advice tendered by any government, including his own. He has become a "European" official.

*Headquarters of the High Authority of the European Coal
and Steel Community, Luxembourg*

The High Authority is responsible ultimately to the European Parliament, which, though it has no legislative function, can force the members of the High Authority to resign through a vote of censure. Individual deputies of the parliament can submit written questions to the High Authority, which also is obliged to keep the European Parliament informed of its actions. The hope of Monnet and other Europeans is that one day deputies to the European Parliament may be elected directly by the people. Presently they are appointed from the membership of their own national parliaments.

Within the strict confines of coal and steel production the governments of the Six have only limited veto power over the High Authority. But sovereignty over general economic and social policy was retained by the Six, who consult with the High Authority through the Council of Ministers, consisting of one cabinet minister from each national government.

Sometimes this representative may be the foreign minister; at other times the minister of industry, or another, depending on the subject under discussion. In certain fundamental cases the High Authority must gain the approval of the Council of Ministers—that is, of the six governments—before proceeding.

Individuals, firms, or governments may appeal decisions of the High Authority to the Court of Justice, whose decisions then are binding on the Six and cannot be set aside by national parliaments. (This court is an institution of the ECSC, wholly separate from the European Court set up by the Council of Europe.)

All this elaborate machinery of the ECSC might have ground itself dry had not the coal and steel merger proved such a vivid success. In the first ten years of the Community's existence, steel production among the Six rose more than 75 per cent, with output of iron ore and pig iron also soaring. Total trade among the Six in ECSC products rose by 168 per cent during the same period. Within the Community the average steel price rose by 3 per cent during the first ten years, compared with 16 per cent in Britain and 24 per cent in the United States.

These first years of the Community coincided with general economic expansion throughout Europe and not all the credit belongs to ECSC. But without the Coal and Steel Community, progress almost certainly would not have been so rapid nor would prices have been held so steady. Prior to the formation of the ECSC, for example, the Aachen coalfield in north-western Germany sold most of its coal within Germany, that is, within the national market, though Belgium and Holland lay just across the border. After the merger and the disappearance of artificial barriers, the Benelux countries more than doubled their purchase of convenient Aachen coal.

Coal, iron, and steel, in other words, began to flow along their natural channels among the Six, as though national frontiers did not exist—which, in the case of these products, they did not. One result was a sharp reduction in transport costs.

Statistics tell only part of the story, for the ECSC's utility was proved equally in adversity. This was especially clear in the case of coal, which entered into a period of crisis during the first years of the Community's existence. In 1950 coal had supplied 74 per cent of the energy needs of the Six. By 1964 this share had fallen to about 43 per cent, as oil and natural gas rushed to the fore. But what of the hundreds of thousands of coal miners threatened by the decline of coal? Here the High Authority stepped in to cushion the blow, in a way no single government could have done.

At this point the High Authority was dealing not with lumps of coal or bars of steel, but with embittered, often bewildered, men—miners whose eyes stared whitely from their faces after the day's work far underground; men and their families who lived in ugly close-packed towns of red brick, turned black by coal; men, however, who clung with fierce pride to their perilous trade. But pride alone could not stand against the inevitable decline of the coal market. The High Authority, moving with care in an emotional situation, and recognizing that coal production would continue to shrink in Europe, introduced a policy of "readaptation and redevelopment"—that is, co-operation with governments to close down uneconomic mines, reorganize the production of others, create new sources of employment in depressed mining areas, and make certain that no miner went hungry during the process. For Belgium, the hardest-hit area of all, this involved a cutting back of coal production by one-third, from thirty million tons to twenty million tons a year, by 1963.

"No to the closing of a Belgian coal mine."
Belgian miners protest closing of an obsolete mine.

Where necessary, the High Authority artificially kept pit-heads open by isolating the Belgian coal market from normal competition and providing a temporary market for Belgian coal, until alternative sources of employment could be developed. Meanwhile, the High Authority advanced millions of dollars of help to nearly 100,000 Belgian miners. "Tideover" allowances were provided between jobs, paying 90 to 100 per cent of previous earnings during the first four months. Moving costs to new jobs were borne by the Community, as were training charges. Then, once settled in new work, the former miners received Community allowances making their pay equal to their old wages for periods of up to two years. Some of these costs the Belgian Government shared equally with the ECSC.

Throughout the Six as a whole, more than 240,000 miners

have left the depressed coal industry, their transfer eased by the High Authority's readaptation policy. These and other costs, including investment loans and the construction of new houses for coal and steel workers, are financed by a direct tax levied by the High Authority on all coal and steel production throughout the Community. Thus the High Authority pays its own way and is dependent on no government for money. By June 30, 1965, the High Authority will have spent $285,000,000 to help finance the construction of 100,000 new dwellings for coal and steel workers of the Six.

Beyond all these tasks, the High Authority is responsible for drawing up long-range assessments of the coal and steel market in Europe, and for making its surveys available to all parties concerned. Gradually it came to be seen that coal, as one source of energy, could not be considered in isolation, but must be co-ordinated with the production and consumption of other forms of energy, outside the jurisdiction of the

Belgian miners receive job retraining

A Dutch coal miner

High Authority, including oil, natural gas, hydroelectric power, and ultimately atomic energy. To this end, the High Authority co-operated with the executive commissions of the later Common Market and Euratom (the European Atomic Energy Community, to be discussed later) in drawing up a common energy policy for the Six, to be implemented fully by 1970.

A protocol laying down the general lines of this policy was adopted by the six governments in April 1964. This document established a number of goals toward which the Community would work—the supply of energy at inexpensive rates; an assured supply sufficient to cover all needs; a progressive substitution of petroleum products and nuclear energy for "older" sources of energy, meaning coal; price stability; a free choice of the kind of fuel used by the consumer; and fair conditions of competition for the producers of the various types of energy.

As the first supranational organization in Europe, the Coal and Steel Community has been called a bridgehead, a pilot project pointing toward a more complete unity in Europe. Without such a concrete institution, men might reasonably doubt the practicality of union. But the success of ECSC showed that governments could safely yield at least a degree of their national sovereignty, with benefit to all. ECSC became a way station on the long and slippery climb toward the distant goal of unity. That way station, once attained, gave a clearer view of the top.

But there were some yawning pitfalls on the road to unity, as the year 1954 proved. In 1950 the Korean War had broken out and the United States, concerned at the weakness of Europe's defenses, had urged upon its Allies that West Germany, only five years after defeat, should be rearmed. Communist China was aiding the North Koreans against United Nations forces in Korea. France was fighting an anti-Communist war in Indo-China. Might not Russia, under these circumstances, strike in Europe? The North Atlantic Treaty Organization was now in being, but only barely so: with a scant fourteen divisions and four hundred aircraft against the Soviet bloc's two hundred divisions and twenty thousand airplanes. A Soviet division was smaller than its Western counterpart, but even so, the West was gravely disadvantaged. Furthermore, West Germany was not yet a member of NATO, although the first burden of Western defense would fall on the Germans. To Washington it seemed essential to put German soldiers back into uniform.

To many Europeans the logic of this might be persuasive, but the prospect was frightening, so soon after the Nazi terror. In Paris wreaths of fresh flowers still were being laid on sidewalks at the places where Resistance fighters had been killed by German soldiers during the liberation of the city in 1944. In country cemeteries across France bereaved parents tended simple graves whose headstones read: "Here lies a soldier of France, who died for his country."

But beyond these griefs a new element had entered the situation. European unity and the end of old feuds was in the air; the Schuman Plan, striking at the roots of the Franco-German rivalry, had just been announced. Why not, then, it was thought, create a European Army, in which German troops would be neutralized, as it were, through multinational control? On May 27, 1952, after months of consultations, proposals, and counterproposals, the six partners of the ECSC signed the European Defense Community (EDC) Treaty.

The army proposed by this treaty would consist of forty divisions, all wearing a European uniform. Controlling this force would be institutions modeled after those of the ECSC—a nine-member executive Commissariat, a Council of Ministers, a Court, and a Parliament. (These last two would be shared with the ECSC.)

Article 38 of the treaty went further, outlining steps to be taken toward a European political federation. On March 10, 1953, another draft treaty was signed, envisaging a European Political Community, or EPC. This community would be serviced by a range of new institutions, including a parliament whose lower house would be elected directly by the peoples of Europe—a long step beyond the practice even of the ECSC assembly. Within two years, according to the draft treaty, the institutions of the Coal and Steel Community, the European Defense Community, and the European Political Community would be fused. Europe, in the mind of its planners, was moving swiftly beyond the narrow economic base of coal and steel to embrace politics and defense.

The United States, anxious to strengthen the free world, strongly favored a European Army. The parliaments of West Germany, Belgium, the Netherlands, and Luxembourg approved the treaty of the EDC. This left France and Italy, with the latter hanging back, waiting on the lead of France. It was in Paris that the crisis came.

The Coal and Steel Community had been one thing—involving the cession of limited economic controls. But a European Army would be something else, striking at the very roots of national sovereignty. For this reason the French followers of the redoubtable General de Gaulle opposed the EDC. The powerful Communist Party of France also opposed it, instructed by Moscow to frustrate a project that at once would put guns in the hands of Germans and would bolster NATO. Many French politicians of other parties feared the disproportionate weight of Germany within a European Army. In vain French Premier Pierre Mendes-France pleaded with the Allies for modifications to the EDC Treaty that would placate these foes. He sought also a British pledge to join the European Army, as a counterweight to Germany. Britain, he was told, supported the EDC, would be allied with it, but would not join.

On August 30, 1954, the French National Assembly (lower house of parliament) voted down the EDC, killing the prospect of a European Army. Destroyed at the same time was the proposed European Political Community. Forward motion toward European unity appeared to have been halted in its tracks, stopped by a revival of the nationalistic fears that had bred the old wars. The European Coal and Steel Community now stood alone as a harbinger of the European movement.

On the military side, an alternative arrangement was pieced together, since the problem of rearming Germany still remained. Britain took the lead in grouping seven nations—the six members of ECSC and Britain—in a new mutual defense organization called the Western European Union, or WEU. Its seven members would co-ordinate the levels of their armed forces, but without infringing on national sovereignties. This would be the framework, much looser than EDC, within which West Germany would be allowed to rearm.

To reassure Europeans, Britain pledged to keep on the Continent four army divisions and a tactical air force. The West German Government provided further assurance by agreeing not to manufacture atomic, biological, or chemical weapons. WEU then assigned force levels to each of its members, including the number of divisions each would put under NATO command. Britain's contribution to NATO would be its four divisions and air force units in Europe. France would supply four divisions, Italy seven, Belgium and Holland two each, and Luxembourg a regimental combat team. West Germany's share would be twelve divisions, much larger than those of its partners, because all West German armed forces would be assigned to NATO, whereas the other members of WEU would retain some units under national command.

Western European Union thus became the route along which West Germany traveled to partnership in NATO. But WEU, like the larger entity of NATO, was simply a co-operative arrangement among sovereign states and did not constitute a step toward European unity. Indeed, that was exactly why the French National Assembly had accepted the Western European Union after rejecting the EDC.

If the stalled European movement was to regain its momentum, the impetus must come from a different quarter. "I am more interested in Europe than in coal and steel." These had been the words of Jean Monnet, on first accepting the presidency of the High Authority of the Coal and Steel Community. Now, following the stunning defeat of the European Army, Monnet resigned his ECSC post, to free his hands for the work that lay ahead.

The Common Market Itself

Existence of the Coal and Steel Community had proved that Europeans would accept economic integration. But the defeat of EDC had shown that Europe, or at least that portion of it represented by the parliament of France, was not ready to accept political integration. To Monnet it seemed clear, in the wake of the EDC debacle, that zeal had outstripped wisdom and that wisdom now must go back and start afresh, building from the agreed base of the ECSC. The next goal to be sought must be economic, avoiding the pitfalls of political suspicions and fears.

Behind the scenes Monnet and other European-minded leaders, including Johan Willem Beyen, Foreign Minister of Holland, and Belgian Foreign Minister Paul Henri Spaak, evolved among themselves and within governmental circles the next steps to be taken. Resulting from these discussions was a meeting at Messina, Sicily, in June 1955 of the foreign ministers of the Six, whose first act was to elect René Mayer, a former French premier, to succeed Jean Monnet as president of the High Authority of the ECSC.

More substantively, the Messina conference then set up a

committee, under the chairmanship of Mr. Spaak, to map out a program of action for the further economic integration of Europe. Auguring well for the committee's work was the election in January 1956 of a French National Assembly more integration-minded than its predecessor.

Separately, Jean Monnet announced the formation in October 1955 of a new organization—the Action Committee for a United States of Europe—which from then on would become Monnet's chief vehicle for guiding the progress of the European movement. The purpose of this unofficial committee was to mobilize, well in advance of parliamentary votes, solid political and trade union support for each forward step toward European unity. To this end Monnet invited thirty-three European politicians and labor leaders, representing all six ECSC nations and most of their political parties and labor unions except the Communists, the Gaullists of France, and parties of the far right, to join his new committee on behalf of their organizations.

Shrewdly, Monnet invited not only advocates of unity, but opponents also. For example, the West German Social Democratic Party had opposed both the Coal and Steel Community and the European Army. Yet Erich Ollenhauer, leader of this German party, accepted membership in Monnet's new committee. From Ollenhauer's point of view, membership in the Action Committee would give him and his party more firsthand information of European plans and programs than he could hope to learn from the West German Government. Monnet, on the other hand, hoped to disarm the suspicions of the Social Democrats before they were called upon to vote again on a European project in the West German Bundestag (lower house of parliament).

Each political party or trade union whose leader was invited to join the Action Committee approved the choice of its own delegate, authorized to speak for thousands of men and women back home in West Germany, Holland, Italy, or elsewhere. Each delegate then pledged himself to support whatever decisions were reached by the Action Committee in its discussions. Around the Action Committee's table sat thirty-three individuals who in fact represented a majority of political and labor union opinion throughout the Six. Represented at that table, for example, were more than twelve million European workers.

In a pleasantly Old World apartment on the tree-lined Avenue Foch in Paris, Monnet and a small personal staff hammered out draft resolutions to be discussed by the Action Committee as a whole. In this way Monnet provided the directing spark for the committee's work.

Perhaps twice a year, more often when the occasion demanded, the committee met in plenary session. Drafts prepared by Monnet and his staff were argued, altered, voted, until finally an "attitude" of the full committee had been achieved. This "attitude" the delegates then took home and tried to implement through their national parliaments, via their political parties and labor unions. As an aide of Monnet expressed it, the Action Committee became the "kernel of organized political backing for specific European proposals."

The first task of his Action Committee, as Monnet saw it, was to mobilize public opinion in favor of the exploratory work being accomplished by the committee headed by Paul Henri Spaak, which, after its establishment by the Messina conference, had begun meeting at the Château de Val Duchesse outside Brussels, capital of Belgium. The Spaak Committee was drawing up integration plans in two fields—atomic energy (which seemed a logical extension of the existing partnership in coal and steel) and an "economic community," to embrace virtually the whole range of industry and agriculture, outside coal, steel, and the atom.

On March 13, 1956, Spaak reported the results of his committee's work to a special session of the Common Assembly of the ECSC, sitting in Brussels. The next month, on April 21, the Spaak Committee sent its formal report to the foreign ministers of the Six. These latter, meeting at Venice on May 29, approved the report and directed the Spaak Committee to write up its conclusions in the form of treaties.

This task was to prove herculean, for the Common Market treaty alone in its final form contained 248 articles, plus protocols and appendices. Finally, on March 25, 1957, two treaties were ready for signing in Rome by the foreign ministers of the Six. One of these treaties established a European Atomic Energy Community (Euratom). The second, far more famous and generally referred to as the Treaty of Rome, set up a European Economic Community (EEC, or Common Market). By year's end the parliaments of all six nations had ratified the treaties, by majorities larger than had approved the Coal and Steel Community. On January 1, 1958, the Common Market and Euratom came into being.

These bare bones of dates hint little of the long months of often agonized debate, as members of the Spaak Committee held in their hands, as it were, the economic future of their peoples and nations. Nor do the dates imply the profoundly important role the Common Market was destined to play, not only among its members, but in relation to the whole trading world. Establishment of the Common Market was like a stone cast into a pool whose widening ripples, mounting into waves, were to rock the policies of many a government, first of all that of Britain.

Signing of the Treaty of Rome signified that "Europe" had been relaunched. But the treaty itself was only a blueprint, charting the community that now must be built, step by step. The eventual economic community, or trading unit, foreseen by the Treaty of Rome would embrace 170,000,000 consumers, the peoples of France, West Germany, Italy, Belgium, the Netherlands, and Luxembourg.[1] The active working population of this community, 74,000,000 people, was larger than that of the United States. Together, these six nations of the EEC formed the world's largest importing unit and its second largest exporter of goods. In 1961 the Common Market was the largest producer of milk in the world, third largest producer of meat. As a unit, the Common Market was second only to the United States in its production of steel and automobiles. Clearly, a single integrated market among the Six would make the Common Market one of the world's three economic giants, along with the United States and the Soviet Union.

The question was, How to attain this integrated market? First of all, the Common Market was to become a customs union. That is, among the six partners themselves tariffs and other artificial restrictions to trade were to be progressively removed until goods and services flowed without impediment among the Six, just as trade was carried on among the states of the United States. (A customs duty, or tariff, is a percentage of the value of a product, like a refrigerator, charged by the

[1] Country	Area in Square Miles	Population in 1960
FRANCE	212,000	45,500,000
WEST GERMANY	95,000	53,400,000
ITALY	116,000	49,300,000
BELGIUM	12,000	9,200,000
NETHERLANDS	12,500	11,500,000
LUXEMBOURG	1,000	314,000
Total:	448,500	169,214,000
United States	3,600,000	181,000,000
Soviet Union	8,600,000	214,000,000

The active working population of the Six was 74,000,000, compared with 72,000,000 in the United States and 99,000,000 in the Soviet Union.

The Treaty of Rome is signed. Among the signatories are Paul Henri Spaak (extreme left) and Konrad Adenauer (fifth from left).

importing government to protect its domestic manufacturers. The sales price of an American refrigerator in France, for example, includes a customs duty, from which French refrigerators are exempt. Similarly, the United States Government charges customs duties on many goods imported into the United States, to protect American manufacturers.)

To eliminate customs duties alone would not be enough. Quota restrictions—that is, limitations on the amounts of any particular product that might cross national frontiers— also had to disappear among the Six. Finally, there must be freedom of circulation for investment capital within the Common Market and also for workers, allowing them to move freely from country to country in response to the shifting demands of an integrated market.

These vast changes, amounting to the dismantling of national economic barriers carefully nurtured over centuries, could not be accomplished overnight. Thus the Treaty of Rome provided for a transitional period of twelve years, divided into three four-year stages, during which customs duties and other restrictions would be progressively reduced until, in 1970, a full common market had been achieved.

Stage one, lasting from 1958 to the end of 1961, originally called for customs duties among the Six to be lowered by 30 per cent and for internal quota restrictions to be reduced by 60 per cent. So successful did the Common Market prove in practice that twice during stage one the Council of Ministers voted to speed up the process. By the end of stage one, internal tariffs had been cut by 40 per cent and quota restrictions on industrial goods had been totally abolished, a goal the Treaty of Rome had not foreseen until 1970. By early 1964 internal customs duties had been reduced by 60 per cent, with Common Market authorities pressing for total abolition by the end of 1966, three years ahead of schedule.

I had a practical illustration of how this worked. In 1961, I moved to France and bought a French automobile. Three years later I moved from France to West Germany and inquired about taking my French car with me. Because this car had been manufactured within the Common Market area, I would have paid only 2.5 per cent of its value as a customs duty on entering Germany. Had that car been British or American—that is, of non-Common Market origin—the West German Government would have charged 20 per cent of its value as import duty. (Had the move from France to West Germany been made after the Common Market had eliminated all internal duties, there would have been no customs charge on a French car at all.)

A customs union implies also a common external tariff,

raised uniformly against the imports of all countries outside the customs union area. This meant that the Six had to align, again by stages, their various national tariffs into a common tariff wall against the outside world. Traditionally France and Italy had been high-tariff lands and the Benelux nations low. Had this condition continued to prevail, foreign goods would have sought to enter the Common Market through low-tariff channels, avoiding France and Italy. This would have distorted artificially the whole pattern of Common Market trade. The solution was to strike an arithmetical average of the national tariffs of the Six, as they existed on January 1, 1957, and align the various national tariffs on this target by degrees until a common external tariff had been reached by 1970. Common Market authorities hope this timetable may be speeded up, to match the progress made in cutting internal duties.

Original plans would have produced a common external tariff generally lower than the tariff structures of Britain and the United States. But the Common Market indicated its willingness to make further concessions, in return for reciprocal tariff cuts by outside governments. The Community took a lead in 1961 by offering a 20 per cent across-the-board reduction in its eventual common external tariff, to which the United States responded by granting reciprocal cuts in many American tariffs.

Like the United States, the Common Market is pledged to pursue a liberal trade policy and the final level of the common external tariff will be decided by world-wide negotiations. These will be conducted primarily through the General Agreement on Tariffs and Trade (GATT), an organization to which most of the world's non-Communist trading nations belong and within which the Six negotiate as a unit.

More delicate than the question of tariffs is the vaster

problem of merging six economies into one, a goal to which the Treaty of Rome was committed, but which could only be accomplished by infringing on the prerogatives of national governments. Economic and social laws in many cases would have to be changed, so that farmers, workers, and manufacturers in each country of the Six could compete on equal terms with those in other member lands. Conditions of competition, in other words, must be harmonized within the Common Market. Inevitably, some less efficient firms and people would be hurt in the process. But the over-all result for 170,000,000 consumers would be a wider flow of better goods, uninhibited by the protectionist policies of individual governments.

In the spring of 1964 the rough spur of inflation prodded the Six faster along this road of integration than had been expected. In France retail prices had risen more than 25 per cent since 1958. Prosperity had virtually eliminated unemployment, with the result that factories competed for workers by offering higher and higher wages. This in turn increased production costs, some of which were passed on to the consumer. Other workers then clamored—and often struck—for more money, in order to cope with rising prices.

Rents in particular had soared spectacularly high, because housing was scarce and more people had money to bargain for a better place to live. My family and I moved to France in the midst of this inflation. We looked at a homely old house in a green and pleasant suburb of Paris. Paint had peeled and chipped from its outside concrete walls. Inside, some of the floors were sinking; the plumbing and wiring were antiquated, as was the small coal furnace that heated the house. A few pieces of old furniture adorned the rooms, making it, technically, a "furnished" house. The rent, the landlady told us blandly, was three hundred dollars a month.

No, she said, she would not fix up the house and, as a matter of fact, the rent would be raised at the end of a year. So we struck a bargain. With our own money we would have the walls and ceilings repainted, the floors sanded and varnished, and a new electrical system installed. The landlady, for her part, agreed not to raise the rent for three years.

The average dwelling unit in France at that time, the early 1960's, was one hundred years old. Ever since the war the French population had been growing, adding to the pressure for housing. Then in 1962 and 1963 came an influx of nearly one million Europeans from Algeria. Houses no better than ours were selling in our town for fifty thousand dollars and more. Rents had climbed beyond the level we were paying. We felt we had done well.

In Italy the inflationary spiral was equally steep, in Belgium and Holland less so, in West Germany least of all. But the Common Market, by lowering economic barriers among the Six, had made inflation "catching." So the West Germans in particular pressed for remedial action to be taken among the Six, even though this meant probing the internal policies of member governments.

The other partners agreed and a "warning system" was set up, in the form of three committees, composed of banking, treasury, and economic officials of each government. One of these committees was charged with drawing up a common budgetary policy for the Six, under which each member government pledged, at least in principle, to conform its yearly budget to recommendations laid down by the Six. These recommendations guarded against excessive spending by any single government, against the accumulation of too large cash reserves, and, conversely, against too large deficits in a country's balance of payments. (A nation's balance of payments is favorable if its total sales of goods and services is larger than

Robert Marjolin, a vice-president of the Common Market Commission

the total value of its imports. If the balance runs the other way, a nation is operating "in the red.") The six governments were urged not to let their public spending outstrip the rate at which their economies were growing. Otherwise too much money would be competing for limited goods, services, and materials, forcing up prices.

A second committee was to co-operate with the Executive Commission of the Common Market in designing an economic policy to extend over the next five years. The groundwork for such a "medium-term economic policy" already had been laid down by Robert Marjolin, a Frenchman who was vice-president and chief economist of the Executive Commission of the EEC.

Experts, according to Mr. Marjolin's plan, would estimate the growth potential of the Common Market over a five-year period, ending in 1970. Guidelines then would be set up for achieving this growth and keeping it in balance, so that no one country or sector of the economy fell out of step. Government spending programs would be tailored to meet the guidelines.

This last was the revolutionary part, for in each country of the Six the government was the largest single enterprise, or employer, controlling railroads, electricity, gas, telephones, airlines, atomic energy, and often large banks, insurance companies, and manufacturing plants. By agreeing to conform their spending programs to international requirements, the member governments in effect were accepting a supranational watchdog over economic and social policy. This was a start toward political unity among the Six.

The third committee set up under the "warning system" was composed of governors of the central banks of the Six. Their job was to help co-ordinate monetary policy and to seek consultation before a member government changed its exchange rate or credit policy.

None of this "warning system" against inflation was aimed at interfering with free enterprise or normal competition among private businessmen within the Community. The EEC's role with regard to private enterprise was to harmonize conditions of competition within the Common Market, so that each businessman had a fair start in the race.

As the decade of the 1960's wore on, the Common Market was rapidly becoming a customs union and less rapidly, but none the less surely, merging six economies into one. Meanwhile, the economic results of these operations of the Common Market were encouraging. From 1957 through 1963, a period which included the first six years of the Community's existence, the gross national product of the Six (their total output of goods and services) increased by 34 per cent. This compared with 16 per cent in Britain and 21 per cent in the United States. The Community's production of industrial goods alone rose by 29 per cent during the first four years of the Common Market, while the comparable figure was 13 per cent in Britain and a bit over 18 per cent in the United States.

Like the earlier Coal and Steel Community, the Common Market had been born in an era of general European prosperity and to some extent the separate economies of the Six would have strengthened on their own. But certain growth factors seemed attributable to the Common Market alone.

Spurred by the lowering of tariffs, trade within the Community had expanded by 130 per cent in the first six years of the EEC's existence. France had increased its exports to the Six by 170 per cent; Italy's sales within the Community had soared by 194 per cent. In 1958 Italy had sold only $608,-000,000 worth of goods to its five partners. In 1963 Italian exports to the EEC amounted to $1,788,000,000. West Germany's exports to the Six had climbed from $2,406,000,000 in 1958 to $5,279,000,000 in 1963, a rise of 119 per cent. Obviously, manufacturers within the Six increasingly were gearing their production, advertising, and sales programs to the giant market provided by the EEC.

Foreign investment capital was flowing rapidly into the Common Market, attracted by the growth prospects of the world's fastest-growing trading unit. Hundreds of American firms, for example, were setting up new factories or licensing and marketing operations within the Common Market, partly to have a foot inside the Community's external tariff wall. From their near-bankrupt status after the war, the Six by 1962 had gold and dollar reserves worth sixteen billion dollars. France and West Germany especially were adding to their reserves.

By the early 1960's President Kennedy was sending American economists to Europe to discover why the Common Market was outstripping the United States in rate of growth. Most governments of the Six, the economists noted, were plowing back into new plant and equipment a significantly higher proportion of their gross national product than was the United States and also were devoting proportionately greater resources to the technical training of youth.

None of this progress would have been possible without the creation of special institutions to administer the Common Market. With two of these institutions, the European Parliament and the Court of Justice, we are already familiar. With the creation of Euratom and the Common Market in 1958, the Common Assembly of the Coal and Steel Community was expanded to 142 deputies and became the European Parliament for all three communities.

Its deputies still are not directly elected, nor do they have a legislative function. Over the Council of Ministers they have no authority. But the European Parliament does retain power to vote out of office the High Authority and the Executive Commissions of the three communities. Also, the parliament exerts indirect influence on Community affairs through its incisive debates, resulting often in improvements in proposals which the Community later enacts into law.

Like the parliament, the Court of Justice of the ECSC expanded its role in 1958 to become the court of last appeal for all three communities, its judgments being final among the Six. Just as the Supreme Court of the United States interprets the American Constitution, so the European Court of Justice is the supreme interpreter of the treaties that brought the European Economic Community into being.

We also will recall the Council of Ministers, as an institution of the European Coal and Steel Community. This Council, comprising one or more ministers from each government, changing according to the subject under discussion, serves also the Common Market and Euratom. But the part the ministers play within the Common Market is distinctly different from their role within the ECSC.

The latter organization had dealt only with coal and steel and the Six governments had given the broad powers of decision to the High Authority of the ECSC. Over some decisions of the High Authority the governments retained veto power, through the Council of Ministers. But in the main the High Authority acted as a supranational director of the coal and steel industries of the Six.

The Common Market, by contrast, embraced the entire national economies of the Six and the governments refused to yield their power of decision to a supranational organization. It would be the governments, and not a "high authority," that would implement the Treaty of Rome and the governments would work through the Council of Ministers. The ministers, however, would act only on specific proposals brought before them by the Common Market Commission.

This nine-man Commission was the executive body of the Common Market, corresponding to the High Authority of the Coal and Steel Community. Men appointed to the Common Market Commission were nationals of the Six, but, like the members of the High Authority, they swore to work only in the Community's interests. Named as the first President of the Common Market Commission was Walter Hallstein, a law professor and former West German Secretary of State for Foreign Affairs, who had represented his government both in the ECSC and Common Market negotiations. Of the Commission's nine members, two each came from France, West Germany, and Italy, and one each from Belgium, Holland, and Luxembourg. Each commissioner, in

Walter Hallstein, first president of the Common Market Commission

addition to his general responsibilities as a member of the executive body of the Common Market, was charged with overseeing progress in some particular economic area in which he was expert, such as agriculture, fiscal policy, or transport.

These nine men preside over a secretariat of about three thousand persons, whose many-faceted task is to research, develop, guide, and administer the Community through its transitional stages into a full-fledged Common Market. These thousands of men and women work in several buildings scattered throughout Brussels, provisional headquarters of the Common Market. The most striking of these buildings is a gleaming structure of white stone and metal, appropriately located on the Avenue de la Joyeuse Entrée, or Street of the Joyous Entry. Here, stretching along labyrinthine halls

*The headquarters of the Common Market in Brussels is
appropriately located on the Avenue de la
Joyeuse Entrée (Street of the Joyous Entry)*

like those of a giant corporation, are the offices of President
Hallstein, the other eight commissioners, and their staffs.

On the top floor of this building is a cafeteria, open only
to EEC employees, which somehow symbolizes the European
character of the Common Market. Signs in the restaurant
are printed in the four official languages of the Community,
French, German, Italian, and Dutch—a provision which
would seem unnecessary. Every one of the hundreds of persons who takes his tray along the daily luncheon line speaks
at least two languages and often three, four, or five. Conver-
sation in the line or at the tables slips naturally from one
tongue to another, as Frenchmen, Germans, Italians, and
Dutchmen mingle.

English is not one of the Community languages. Yet an American or British visitor would have no difficulty in being understood, for most of the upper grade employees speak English in addition to their Community tongues. Every person hired by the Community is required to speak at least two of its languages and preferably more. Set high on a hill overlooking the bustling city of Brussels, Common Market headquarters might be likened to a modern Tower of Babel.

These "Eurocrats," as Community civil servants inevitably were nicknamed, form an intellectual elite, a kind of European nationality administering the affairs of the Six. The total of Community employees in all three institutions (Coal and Steel, Euratom, and Common Market) is about seven thousand. These Community workers no longer pay national income taxes to their own governments, but a special European tax directly to the EEC. Those "Eurocrats" stationed in Brussels receive distinctive license plates for their cars—the letters EUR surrounded by six stars, plus a number.

EEC employees have special license plates

This sign is at a European Community School in Brussels

Already the children of Community families are perpetu-
ating the European tradition by attending one of six "European schools," especially created for the EEC. History and
geography, in fact all subjects, are taught from a European
standpoint, free of national bias. Each child works from the
beginning with two languages, his own and either French or
German. Starting with the seventh grade, all students are
required to study Latin. The next year they begin English.
These students graduate from the equivalent of high school
with a "European diploma," recognized by the universities
of the Six and by those of Austria.

The three communities finance the schools, which are
administered by the ministers of education in the countries
in which they are located. Expressing the spirit of the Euro-

Students at the European Community School in Varese-Ispra, Italy

pean schools is the following statement, sealed into the foundation stones of two of the schools, one at Luxembourg City and the other at Varese-Ispra, Italy.

"Being brought up in contact with each other and freed at an early age from the prejudices which divide, initiated into the beauties and values of the various cultures, they will as they grow up become conscious of their solidarity. While retaining love for and pride in their country, they will become in spirit Europeans well prepared to complete and consolidate the work undertaken by their fathers to establish a prosperous and united Europe."

Since the Common Market Commission cannot legislate decisions on its own, it has in one sense less power than the High Authority of the ECSC. But in another sense it was given more power, for the High Authority dealt only with coal and steel, whereas the Commission was charged with charting progressively the complete economic integration of the Six. As each provision of the Treaty of Rome falls due for implementation, it is the Common Market Commission which draws up detailed working plans to be voted into law by the Council of Ministers. The Commission formulates its proposals only after prolonged consultations, lasting often for months, with everyone who will be affected by the proposal— the six governments themselves, their business and professional groups, and labor unions. The result is a synthesis which, while adhering strictly to the provisions of the Treaty of Rome, takes everyone's interests into account. The final proposal, shaped and polished into a detailed text, is presented by the Commission to the Council of Ministers to be voted into law, binding on the Six.

The ministers, before taking their vote, consult the European Parliament for an "opinion" and also a 101-member Economic and Social Committee. This Committee was provided for by the Treaty of Rome to focus and make available the representative views of business, labor, and professional elements among the Six. Like the Parliament, the Economic and Social Committee can only advise. But the 101 members of this Committee, appointed by the Council of Ministers after nomination by their national governments, provide a spectrum of opinion which the ministers and the Commission very much need.

Institutionally, then, the Common Market has an executive Commission, responsible for implementing the Treaty of Rome through specific proposals; a Council of Ministers, which turns these proposals into law; a European Parliament and an Economic and Social Committee, which play consultative roles; and a Court of Justice, the final arbiter of the

Treaty of Rome. Representing the Council of Ministers in Brussels is a Committee of Permanent Representatives, whose members have ambassadorial rank and act as on the spot delegates of the six national governments. Three other consultative committees established by the Treaty of Rome advise the Commission and Council of Ministers on monetary, trade-cycle, and transport problems.

Time has proven the nine-man Commission headed by Professor Hallstein to be the creative spark of this administrative complex. Though the Council of Ministers retains legislative power, it can act in most cases only on recommendations made by the Commission. The concrete shape, tone, and color of the evolving Common Market are determined first of all by the Commission, which also acts as a watchdog over progress already achieved. Increasingly the six governments tend to look upon the Commission as the "management team" of the Common Market. Significantly, it was to the Commission and not to the Council of Ministers that the six governments were asked to report their budget-making policies, after the anti-inflation warning system was set up in 1964. Less openly supranational than the High Authority of the ECSC, the Common Market Commission in fact casts a far wider shadow of influence over Europe as a whole.

As the Common Market passes through its transitional stages, the six governments progressively lose some of their veto powers. It required a unanimous vote of the Council of Ministers to pass the Community from stage one to stage two at the end of 1961. This vote involved a heart-searching struggle, as will be seen in the next chapter. But the vote was taken, stage two was entered, and in the process the member governments knowingly surrendered a bit of their sovereignty. It will take, for example, only a qualified majority vote to

Belgian workers return from their day's work in France.
Eventually there will be a ceasing of frontier formalities.

pass the Common Market from its second to third stage, which means that no single member government any longer can block by veto the forward movement of the Community.

Stage one concentrated on the removal of restrictions on trade among the Six, such as customs and quotas. Stage two involves giant steps beyond a mere customs union toward the merging of the six economies into one. Among other things, stage two, which runs to the end of 1965, requires the Six to equalize the wages of men and women workers. This will entail changes in national legislation; indeed, in the whole social outlook of peoples. A European Labor Exchange will be established in Brussels, to co-ordinate job vacancies and opportunities among the Six, a task hitherto restricted to national governments, acting within their own frontiers.

Equally important, a wider variety of questions is decided by qualified, or weighted, majority during the second stage. Under the qualified majority system of voting, each member state is given weighted votes, roughly proportionate to its population. France, Italy, and West Germany each have four votes, Belgium and the Netherlands two each, and Luxembourg one. This makes a total of seventeen. A minimum of twelve votes is required to decide on a proposal by the Commission, which means that no single government, even the largest, can torpedo a measure approved by its partners. In the rarer case when the Council of Ministers is acting on a measure of its own, the twelve votes must include at least four member states.

Even in stage two, the governments retained the unanimity rule on certain fundamental matters, including the admission to the Common Market of new members or associated states, the control of international trade negotiations between the Community and outside powers, and the harmonization of basic social, fiscal, and economic policies.

Generally speaking, the area of veto power is narrowing and the area of majority voting is widening as the Community progresses through its transitional stages to the end of 1969, when a full Common Market is due to come into being. (Stage three, which runs from the beginning of 1966 to the end of 1969, can be prolonged for a period of no longer than three years by unanimous vote of the Council of Ministers, acting on a proposal by the Commission.)

Like the earlier Coal and Steel Community, the Treaty of Rome established a resettlement fund, to help finance the retraining of workers dislocated by Common Market developments. This European Social Fund pays half the expenses incurred by member governments on resettlement projects approved by the Common Market Commission.

Another important fund provided for by the Rome treaty was a one billion dollar European Investment Bank, whose primary function is to help member governments develop backward regions of their countries. In its early stages this investment fund was drawn on most heavily by Italy, whose economy lagged generally behind those of its five partners.

When the Treaty of Rome was signed in 1957, France was the most important colonial power among the Six. At that time the tricolor flag of France waved over almost four million square miles of African territory, containing nearly forty million people. During the long years of French African empire, millions of Negroes and Arabs had acquired a taste for French culture. Their second language was French and the elite among them came to France for university training. Economic ties between France and Africa were equally strong. The colonies sent their cocoa, coffee, copra, cotton, wine, sisal, and peanuts to France, in exchange for French manufactured goods.

But Africa was on the march toward independence in 1957. Already Tunisia and Morocco had gained their freedom from France, and the French Government had set in motion a vast program of increased autonomy, leading toward the independence of all its colonies and trust territories south of the Sahara. In 1958 Guinea became free, followed in 1960 by fourteen other French African colonies and territories. In 1962 the process of independence was completed, when Algeria became a sovereign republic.

The French African empire was a thing of the past. But cultural and economic ties, important to both sides, persisted. Thousands of French teachers still work in the former colonies, ten thousand of them in Algeria, Tunisia, and Morocco alone. Hundreds of slim black young men, students at the University of Paris, crowd the Latin Quarter of the

French capital, speaking impeccable French in soft African tones. Every day bewildered Arabs from Algeria stumble ashore at Marseilles, clutching their belongings in cloth bundles and bags. They have come to work in France, to earn money to send back to their families in the homeland. Each year France pumps half a billion dollars of aid—economic, technical, and military—into its former Negro colonies south of the Sahara. Another large amount goes to the former North African dependencies of Algeria, Tunisia, and Morocco.

France wants very much to keep its influence in Africa. French negotiators had insisted before the Treaty of Rome was signed that the Common Market must include some form of association between the Six and their colonies. Otherwise, it was argued, the customs union provision of the Treaty of Rome would oblige France to give up its preferential treatment of its colonies' crops. This would cause grave hardship in many African lands and might strengthen anti-Western elements among them. The same would be true of Belgian colonies in Africa, notably the giant Congo.

This argument prevailed and the Treaty of Rome provided for a five-year association period between the Six and their colonies. All Six would open their doors equally and on a privileged basis to the exports of the colonies. This allowed dependent territories to slip inside the eventual common external tariff of the Community, giving them an advantage over the world's other exporters of tropical products, such as the countries of Latin America. The colonies, meanwhile, were allowed to retain their tariffs, even against manufactured products of the Six, where these were needed to protect infant industries.

Trade privileges alone were not enough to start the colonies on the road toward economic equilibrium. Thus the Treaty of Rome established a European Development Fund for Overseas (EDF), totaling $581,000,000, to finance the social and economic development of the colonies. France, whose dependent territories were to receive $511,000,000 of this aid, contributed $200,000,000 to the fund. West Germany, with no colonies, contributed a like amount. Nearly half the total fund was spent on what is called "infrastructure" development—the roads, ports, railroads, and other communications facilities which new industries require. The modernization of farming areas absorbed another large amount, as did the building and staffing of various types of schools.

During the five-year association period every one of the territories involved gained its independence. Now the African countries were politically sovereign, but still economically dependent on the Six. All but Guinea, whose relations with France had become troubled during the independence period, chose to remain associated with the Common Market. In July 1963 a new five-year Association Convention was signed between the Six and eighteen independent African states, expanding the provisions of the original agreement.[2]

The Six pledged an additional $730,000,000 in aid funds (38 per cent more than the first time), of which $620,000,000 would be in the form of outright grants. The remainder would be loans for special projects. This fund does not replace national aid programs; France continues to give nearly one billion dollars a year to its former African colonies. During the five-year span of the first association agreement, the Six individually gave nearly seven billion dollars in aid

[2] Fourteen of the eighteen associated African states formerly were governed by France —Cameroun, Central African Republic, Chad, Congo (Brazzaville), Dahomey, Gabon, Ivory Coast, Madagascar, Mali, Mauretania, Niger, Senegal, Togo, and Upper Volta. Three others had been ruled by Belgium—Burundi, Congo (Leopoldville), and Rwanda, while the eighteenth, Somalia, had been under Italian trusteeship.

*Sovereign African states sign a new Association
Convention with the Six, July 1963*

to underdeveloped nations. Of this total, the lion's share
came from France, which has the highest per capita aid program among major powers in the world.

Projects worked out by European and African experts
trickle steadily through Community machinery and are approved. In April 1964 for example, the Common Market
Commission announced the financing of a new drug supply
depot at Nouakchott, capital of Mauretania. At the same
time the Commission approved the provision of pure drink-
ing water for the people of two towns in Guadeloupe, a
Caribbean island which remains under French rule. This
illustrated another aspect of the 1963 Association Convention, which provided an additional $70,000,000 in aid to over-
seas territories still controlled by the Six.

On the trade side, Community tariffs on a number of tropical exports from Africa were abolished altogether. Industrial raw materials already enjoyed free entry into the Common Market. Other exports of the associated African countries benefited from the gradual reduction of internal tariffs among the Six, for the customs union had swelled to include the eighteen African lands. The latter, for their part, pledged in principle to reduce their tariffs on imports from the Six by 15 per cent yearly and to abolish quota restrictions on these imports. They retained, however, the right to maintain tariffs where necessary to protect their budding industries.

This continuing association of eighteen African countries with the Six is important to the entire free world, for, in an age of revolutionary ferment, it tends to keep the leaders of those countries oriented toward the West. Economic benefits derived by the eighteen from their association with the Common Market undercuts communism in Africa. So successfully is the Association Convention working out that several other countries, including Nigeria, Kenya, and Uganda, have asked to discuss similar arrangements with the Six, when the present convention expires in 1968.

Latin American and other underdeveloped nations have complained that their primary crop exports are bound to lose ground in the Common Market, against the competition of duty-free exports from Africa. Recognizing this, the Six agreed to slash their duties on similar products coming from the outside world. But a final solution to this problem awaits world-wide commodity agreements among trading nations, within a framework far wider than the EEC alone. Among the Six, the Dutch and West Germans have pressed for an extension of the preferential system to embrace all underdeveloped lands. With no former colonial ties in Africa, West Germany and the Netherlands traditionally have bought many tropical imports from Latin America.

Some African governments outside the eighteen have rejected Community association as an extension of colonialism. Others, such as Tunisia, Morocco, and Algeria, the former French dependencies in North Africa, still are exploring their way toward a permanent relationship with the EEC. Special clauses in the Treaty of Rome allow these three nations to retain some of their preferential trading arrangements with France until 1970. By that time they must decide on a firm relationship. Their trade is mostly with the Six and this fact seems likely to push Tunisia, Morocco, and Algeria into some form of EEC orbit.

African countries, however friendly, cannot hope to become full members of the EEC, since they lie outside Europe. Article 238 of the Treaty of Rome specifies that "Any European State may ask to become a member of the Community. It shall address its application to the Council which after taking the advice of the Commission decides unanimously." Certain European governments, notably that of Britain, have applied for membership, as will be seen in a later chapter. But there were other smaller, more backward, European states, not yet qualified for full membership, whose trade was vitally affected by the development of the EEC. To such countries the Community held out the prospect of association, leading possibly to later membership.

Greece was the first nation to take advantage of this formula. On November 1, 1962, after nearly two years of hard negotiations, an association agreement between Greece and the EEC came into force. A customs union was to be gradually established over a long transitional period of twenty-two years, during which the Greek economy was to be systematically developed toward a competitive status with the more advanced economies of the Six. To accomplish this the Six agreed to provide Greece with $125,000,000 worth of financial aid through the European Investment Bank. Simultaneously, a development aid consortium to help Greece was formed among several members, including the United States, of the twenty-nation Organization for Economic Co-operation and Development. At the end of 1984, it was hoped, Greece would be ready for full membership in the EEC.

Turkey was the second European nation to work out a long-term relationship with the Common Market. Over a period of five years, beginning in 1963, the Six agreed to furnish Turkey with $175,000,000 in credits, designed to strengthen the Turkish economy to the point that Turkey would be ready for associate membership, similar to that achieved by Greece. An OECD aid consortium for Turkey also was formed. At the end of the five-year "preparatory period," which can be extended to nine years, Turkey is scheduled to enter a twelve-year transitional period, leading to a full customs union with the EEC. "Signature of this agreement," declared the Turkish foreign minister, "links our destiny irreversibly with that of Europe."

Spain, by contrast, was turned down for associate membership with the Six, on the grounds that the authoritarian government of Generalissimo Franco was not democratic—an essential requirement for membership in the Common Market. In June 1964 the Six finally agreed to open economic discussions with Spain, though not necessarily as a prelude to membership.

Iran and Israel illustrated the situation of nations which had not been colonies of the Six, did not belong to Europe, could not, therefore, qualify for any kind of membership, and yet ran heavy trading deficits with the Common Market. Israel, for example, sold goods worth $60,000,000 yearly to the Six, but bought in return goods worth $140,000,000, a great deal of red ink for a country as small as Israel. To ease the trading problems of Israel and Iran, the Common Market in 1964 concluded special agreements with them, granting tariff concessions on a wide range of products exported by the two Middle Eastern states.

Already the sights of the Six have been lifted far beyond a simple customs union among them, even beyond the more demanding challenge of a full economic merger. The impact of this developing community of 170,000,000 persons is causing major repercussions throughout the world. Britain, as will be seen, reversed an attitude of centuries and in 1961 knocked on the door of Europe. A large part of Africa has linked itself with the Common Market. Two nations on the eastern fringe of Europe have obtained different degrees of associate status. Countries outside Europe and Africa are seeking special relationships. The emergence of a new trading giant, shouldering its way toward equality with the United States and Russia, is a world-wide phenomenon, extending its influence far beyond the Six, who started only a few years before by pooling their coal and steel.

Farmers and the Common Market

Along a straight, tree-lined French road between Chartres and Orleans walked a stout peasant woman, carrying a gunny sack of greens slung over one shoulder. In her other hand she carried an empty bucket and a rude staff, fashioned from a tree branch. She had been out collecting wild salad greens, to be cooked into the soup stock which almost always simmered in a huge kettle on the back of her stove.

Once she stopped, put down her sack, and shifted burdens from hand to hand before plodding on in her heavy work shoes. Far down the road she turned in toward a clump of trees, which masked the small French farmstead where she lived. The farmhouse was long and low, connected to a wattled barn by walls made of dried mud and wood. The woman saw her husband standing in the open doorway of the house, arguing with a man dressed in city clothes. For a moment she stopped and listened. Then she shrugged, put down her load, and fell to hoeing the first bright green lettuces of spring, growing in a garden patch beside the house.

The elderly farmer at the door was shaking his head angrily at the man from the city. "This land was my father's, and his father's, and his grandfather's before that!" the farmer said hotly. "I will not give it up!"

"Mon vieux," repeated the government agent patiently, "in return you would receive a larger and better piece, attached to your main farm. It is too expensive for you to farm this separate plot, a kilometer away."

"Do you tell me how to farm, too?" the farmer muttered, and the agent shrugged helplessly and went away.

He had tried to persuade two neighboring farmers, who had inherited checkerboards of divided plots, to exchange two pieces of land and thus gain wholly contiguous farms. One farmer had agreed; the old man had not. As a result both would continue to waste time and effort hauling equipment and material between isolated plots of land. Both would remain far behind factory workers in their region in income earned. Even had they agreed to realign their plots, their farms would have remained small, among that 79 per cent of French farms less than seventy acres large—the average minimum which the French Government considers economically profitable in France.

The peasants of France are an ancient lot, whose roots in the land go back to the Roman occupation of Gaul and even before, to the Celtic stock of the country. Some French farming families claim to trace their ownership of a particular piece of land back to the days of Charlemagne; and just as the Frankish custom of dividing the inheritance destroyed the unity of the Frankish empire, so the peasant fathers of Gaul and later of France split up their farms to give them to their sons. The result was a patchwork of farm ownership, which today from the air looks like a crazy quilt of greens and browns, over which crawl horses, men, and tractors.

This problem is not unique to France among the countries of the Common Market. A study published in 1963 by the

Aerial view of the French farmland

OECD showed the condition to be universal among the Six. Nearly 70 per cent of Belgian farms were less than twenty-five acres large, far below the profitable minimum, and fragmentation into divided plots was common among these. The story was the same in West Germany, where 72 per cent of the farms were smaller than twenty-five acres. In Holland the equivalent figure was 60 per cent, in Luxembourg 40 per cent. In Italy the situation was worst of all. Nearly 90 per cent of Italian farms were found by the OECD to be less than twenty-five acres in size. A majority of Common Market farmers, in other words, could not make an adequate living from their land.

Inevitably, in every country of the Six, this led to a maze of government price support regulations, designed to make it possible for farmers and their families to exist. For many crops and dairy products the government set "price floors," varying often from year to year according to market conditions. If the farmer's selling price for milk, wheat, or meat fell below this floor, the government made up the difference to him in cash. Governments also protected the farmer from foreign competition by erecting tariff or quota restrictions against the importation of farm goods. This was the situation prevailing, when the Common Market came into being in 1958.

For the governments of the Six their farm problems were politically explosive, for farmers made up a considerable proportion of the population in most Common Market countries. Fourteen per cent of West German people earned their living wholly or partly from the land. The figure was 20 per cent in France, 30 per cent in Italy. (This contrasted with 4 per cent in Britain, 6 per cent in the United States.) These millions of Common Market farmers made up voting blocs, potentially able to tip the balance for or against a political party at election time.

The contrast between the income of farm and factory workers was exposed by the so-called Green Report for 1964 issued by the West German Government. Each person employed on about eight thousand West German farms had earned an average of $1,161 during the agricultural year 1962–1963. While this had been an increase of 25 per cent over the preceding year, it still was 29 per cent less than factory workers of equivalent skills had earned. The result was a system of government subsidies to German farmers, amounting to well over half a billion dollars a year.

A part of the answer, as the six governments saw it, was to mechanize and modernize their farms, thus reducing the number of men needed to grow the food, while increasing the income of the farmers who remained.

Each year in France, for example, at least 100,000 young men and women leave the nation's farms, lured by the higher rewards of industrial work. This migration is encouraged by the government as long as industry can absorb new workers. In addition, there is a gradual disappearance of older farmers, who—like the peasant and his wife on the road between Chartres and Orleans—tend to be most fixed in antiquated methods. As a result of this tendency, the farm population in France has declined from 27 to 20 per cent of the total since 1955 and the government hopes to push it down at least to 15 per cent.

To accomplish this, the French Government has launched a long-term program of agricultural renovation, based on the conviction that the farming of less than 70 acres by one family no longer can be made economical in France. The program's many parts include the introduction of co-operative farming methods wherever possible, embracing joint use of equipment, realignment of lands, and marketing of products through co-operative producers' groups.

For decades the raucous bustle of Les Halles, the sprawling central market of Paris, has charmed tourists, who have delighted to wander through its crowded stalls and sit down at dawn to eat onion soup. But the tourist may not have realized that the ancient marketing system of France, exemplified by Les Halles, has obliged every French housewife to pay more for her food and caused every French farmer to get less for his crops. Under the time-honored dominance of Les Halles, much of the foodstuff grown in France traditionally has traveled to Paris, to be processed at Les Halles, before being routed to retail markets throughout the nation. The result has been to make the cost of handling food exorbitantly high. French farmers claim that in some cases they receive only one-thirtieth of the price which the consumer finally pays for a head of lettuce or cabbage.

*Les Halles, the colorful market in Paris where most foodstuffs
are processed, will soon be replaced by a new market
on the outskirts of the city*

To end this wasteful system, the French Government is
building a network of regional slaughterhouses and marketing points, aimed at reducing the middleman's role and allowing local foodstuffs to be processed more nearly on the spot.
Les Halles itself, which daily chokes the capital with its army
of food trucks, is being replaced by a gleaming new central
market on the outskirts of Paris.

Other features of the government's program include the
pre-emptive right, through state agencies, to buy up land
which comes on the market, divide it up where it will do the
most good, and resell it on credit to small farmers. Unculti-
vated land on which taxes have not been paid may be taken
by the government and sold. Old farmers who agree may be

pensioned off and young farmers given instruction in modern methods. Since even then much of the French farm population will remain surplus, young men wishing to go into other work will be given training by the state.

Each in its own way, the other governments of the Six are duplicating this program in their own domains. West Germany's Green Report of 1964 noted that the number of Germans employed in agriculture had declined by 42 per cent since 1950, while output per person, due to an extensive program of farm modernization, had risen by 152 per cent. In 1964 the West German Government spent more than $300,000,000 on improving living conditions on the farms and on "structural adjustment" of West German agriculture, including the merging of small farms into larger units, the resettlement of dislocated families, and the construction of new roads in farming communities.

Even so, West German farmers remained the Common Market's supreme example of subsidization, a distinction for which West German consumers paid dearly in high food prices. The average West German family pays out 35 per cent of its income for food, against 19 per cent for a family in the United States. Within the Common Market, West German grain prices—the largest single item in agriculture—are approximately 20 per cent higher than the average grain prices of the other five Community members. These prices will be aligned by July 1967, when a common grain price is due to go into effect among the Six. West Germany's highly protected farmers, and their insistence that they remain protected, are a major reason why the creation of a common market in agriculture has been so difficult for the Six to achieve.

An opposite kind of reason exists in France. On the one hand, as we have seen, thousands of small French farmers are unable to make a living on tiny farms. Yet the soil of

Old-fashioned farming methods still prevail in much of Belgium

France is so rich that over-all the nation produces a surplus of food, more than can be sold. Individual farmers are in hardship, while the cumulative effect of too many farmers working fertile soil has been overabundance. The farm modernization program has added to this part of the problem by boosting crop yield per acre.

In the summer of 1963 the frustrations of French farmers took a violent turn. Angry fruit farmers, burdened by their own bumper crops, destroyed large quantities of Spanish plums, peaches, and tomatoes being sold near Marseilles. Fish from Portugal was scattered on town streets to rot. Further north, French farmers dumped tons of their surplus potatoes in town squares and mashed them to pulp with their tractors.

Later, the farmers changed their tactics. Premier Georges Pompidou and other Cabinet ministers began receiving two-

Mechanized farming in France

pound sacks of potatoes in their mail, to remind the government that French farmers were unhappy. Other farmers near the northwestern town of Beauvais set up "barricades of charm." Pretty farm girls stopped motorists and offered them free butter, sugar, and cheese—along with a tract outlining the farmers' plight. Weekend drivers in southern France found roads blocked by farmers, who poured them free wine and offered them fruit.

Behind these demonstrations lay the marvelous productivity of the well-watered soil of France, which time and again had brought the nation back from the ravages of war and revolution. This was a boon, but by the early 1960's it also had become something of a two-edged sword.

France possessed roughly half the arable land within the six-nation European Economic Community. It was by far the largest food producer among the Six, ranking first in output of wheat and coarse grains, cattle meat, milk, poultry, sugar, and vegetables, and second in potatoes, butter, cheese, eggs, and wool. The small French farm, uneconomic for the proprietor himself, was a comparatively large producer of food. Coupled with this high productivity was the rapid mechanization achieved by some minority sectors of French agriculture since World War II. Certain large dairy farms in Normandy, for example, had become indistinguishable from their most modern counterparts in the United States.

The result of all this was surplus, over and above the exports which had made France the leading food exporter in Western Europe. France urgently needed new markets to absorb its surpluses of grain, dairy products, and sometimes beef, plus seasonal spurts of fruit and vegetable crops. The logical market was close at hand—the nations of the Six.

Foreseeing this, French negotiators had insisted during the long travails of the Spaak Committee in 1956 that the proposed Common Market must include agriculture as well as industry. French industry, they argued, was less efficient than that of West Germany. France was willing to take the risk of industrial competition which the Common Market would imply. But Germany in turn must take the risk of competing with France on the farm. French negotiators, backed up strongly by the Dutch, who had their own farm surpluses to sell, won their point. Agriculture, according to the Treaty of Rome, was to march step by step with industry toward a common market, within which farm goods would circulate freely among the Six, devoid of tariffs, quotas, and other restrictions.

But in fact this did not work out. There was always the stubborn problem that thousands of West German farmers would have been inundated by cheaper imports from France.

West Germany also had commitments to buy foodstuffs from countries which were important customers for German industrial exports. Beyond this was the uncertainty of agriculture, dependent on the vagaries of the weather, which meant that national support prices and other protective devices had to fluctuate from year to year. But the French kept insisting that a goal of the Treaty of Rome was a common market in agriculture, including common support prices and external tariffs, to be levied equally throughout the Six.

A crisis came at the end of 1961, when the Common Market was due to pass from stage one to stage two. The French Government made clear it would exercise its right to block this progress, unless steps had been taken to establish a common policy in agriculture. In effect, this was a threat to end the Common Market, unless West Germany made the concessions required of it by the Treaty of Rome.

In an atmosphere of crisis, with all that had been accomplished by the Six hanging in the balance, the Council of Ministers began to meet, daily, nightly, as 1961 slipped away. Juridically the clock was stopped at the end of the year, to allow the first stage to continue. Finally, at five o'clock on the morning of January 14, 1962, after an exhausting series of forty-five meetings, the Council of Ministers voted unanimously to advance the Common Market to its second state. West Germany had made its sacrifice, or more properly, had accepted the next obligations of the treaty it had signed.

All over Europe people breathed more easily. An essential corner had been turned. By progressing to stage two the governments of the Six had given up some of their veto powers. They scarcely would have done so, it was reasoned, had they not felt themselves committed to the Common Market.

Specifically, the Six had agreed to an agricultural code

which would establish a common market in farm goods over a seven and one-half year preparatory period, from July 1, 1962, to December 31, 1969. The code bristled with technical terms—variable levies, sluicegate prices, threshold prices. But behind this complex verbiage, the code was one of profound and practical meaning to West German farmers on their cold northern plains, to Frenchmen turning up the dark soil of the fertile Beauce, to Italians tending olive groves and vineyards on sun-warmed Mediterranean slopes, to Dutchmen whose level lands stretched away to the sea.

The regulations agreed upon called for the prices of each agricultural product to be gradually harmonized throughout the Six, until a common price level had been established by 1970. The progressive stripping away of trade restrictions among the countries of the Common Market would tend to align these prices through the competitive operation of supply and demand. This was similar to the system already well advanced in the industrial sector of the EEC.

To protect farmers and consumers during the adjustment period, each member country would be allowed to charge a "variable levy" on imported foodstuffs, if these proved cheaper than the home-grown product. That is, if France were able to sell a bunch of carrots in Germany for five cents, while German carrots cost seven cents a bunch, the West German Government would be allowed to charge a two-cent levy on the imported French carrots. Similarly, West German farmers would be paid a Common Market export subsidy, to permit them to offer their carrots competitively in France.

These levies and export subsidies, supervised by the Common Market Commission, were to replace all existing national protective measures, including support prices. Gradually the Common Market levies and subsidies would be reduced over the seven and one-half year preparatory period, until a common price level had been achieved by 1970. This was a vast responsibility for the Common Market Commission to undertake. Yet it seemed the only feasible way to merge six separate markets into one.

Vis-à-vis the outside world, the Six wanted protection and preference for their own farm products, just as they were seeking to protect their industries through the erection of a common external tariff. Thus another system of levies was set up to be imposed on farm imports from outside the Community. These levies would be higher than levies within the Community and also would be permanent, to guarantee preference to Common Market farmers.

President de Gaulle put the matter succinctly when he insisted that the Six should be largely self-sufficient in foodstuffs. This attitude was to cause anguish among food-exporting nations, including the United States, which annually sold more than a billion dollars' worth of farm products to Western Europe.

The regulations agreed upon by the Six also established a European Agricultural Guidance and Guarantee Fund, to finance the operations of the agricultural common market, both in its preparatory and completed stages. Until 1965 this fund was to be made up of contributions from the governments of the Six. After 1965 the fund was to derive its capital from levies charged on agricultural imports from the outside world. An important function of the Guarantee Fund was to buy up internal farm surpluses, over and above Common Market needs, and attempt to sell them outside the Community at world prices.

A safeguard clause was included in the farm regulations, to allow a member country to suspend agricultural imports from its EEC partners, if for some reason its internal market was under severe strain. This clause could be invoked only by notifying the other member governments and the Common Market Commission, which then would make a ruling on the plea. If challenged by the government concerned, the Commission's ruling was to be approved or rejected by the Council of Ministers, voting by weighted majority.

Within this general framework of agricultural rules, various categories of farm products were to march at different paces toward the common market goal. On January 14, 1962, when the Six had committed themselves to a common market in agriculture, the Community also had agreed on specific rules governing trade in grains, pigmeat, eggs and poultry, fruits, vegetables, and wines, which among them accounted for more than half of the EEC's total agricultural production. Five administrative committees, each comprising representatives of the Six, were established to apply these rules progressively toward a common market in these products. Policy on rice, beef, dairy produce, and sugar was to be decided later. Later still would come policy on oils and fats, fish, tobacco, and forestry.

With the exception of grains, the five original committees found the going relatively easy in implementing rules governing pigmeat, poultry products, fruits, vegetables, and wines. Sugar also subscribed to Community rules on schedule. But rice, beef, and dairy produce proved stubborn—or rather, the interests behind them did. Also, the Six were unable to agree on the administration of the European Agricultural Guidance and Guarantee Fund. June 30, 1962, the first deadline established by the January 14 accord, passed without agreement. So did the next deadline proposed, December 31 of that year.

In January 1963 General de Gaulle threw a bombshell into the Community by vetoing Britain's entry into the Common Market. For the moment, agriculture was forgotten in the wake of this larger shock. By springtime, however, the Community had pulled itself together from the General's veto and had turned back to agriculture. On May 9, 1963, the Council of Ministers agreed on the end of that year as a new deadline for settlement of the four outstanding farm problems. If this deadline were not met, President de Gaulle declared in July, the Common Market would "risk disappearing."

Again a flurry in the chancelleries. Did France mean to pull out of the Community? Not at all, French officials explained. But agriculture had fallen behind the timetable all had accepted. French fruits and vegetables were rotting unsold and French farmers were growing violent. The Six had agreed on a common market for agriculture. If regulations governing this were not in place by the end of the year, the Common Market in fact would not exist and would "risk disappearing."

Once again, in December 1963, there were contentious meetings of the Council of Ministers in Brussels. The French in effect pointed an accusing finger at the Germans, as the delegation holding up the progress of the Common Market for nationalistic reasons. The West Germans retorted that the French Government's desire to achieve a solution was just as nationalistic, since the French economy would benefit thereby. But once again, when all that had been achieved seemed threatened, the Six found a way to agree.

Three new market organizations, or committees, were established, to handle rice, dairy products, and beef and veal. These committees joined the five already at work on other farm products. A common agricultural policy for rice became effective September 1, 1964. Regulations for dairy products, beef, and veal followed on November 1. In addition the Six established common regulations for fats and

The agricultural marathon talks in December 1963

oils. Finally, the Council of Ministers adopted general rules for the operation of the Guidance and Guarantee Fund.

The next imposing hurdle had been cleared. Regulations affecting 85 per cent of the Community's farm output had been put in place. Dr. Sicco L. Mansholt, a vice-president of the Common Market Commission and its leading agricultural expert, now set his sights on a common grain price within the Six, as a further step toward implementing a common market for cereals. Grain was central to the whole concept of an agricultural common market. The price of grain was reflected in the price paid in the grocery store for bread and flour. What the housewife paid for beefsteak, bacon, and milk depended in part on the price of animal feed grains.

The grain production of the Six already had been protected from outside competition by the imposition of variable levies on imports. But this left unchanged the sharp price differences existing among the Six themselves. Dr. Mansholt proposed an internal selling price for grain midway between the high of West Germany and the low of France, a solution that seemed inevitable if a common grain price were to be achieved. This solution would have raised grain prices in France and the Netherlands and lowered them in West Germany, Italy, and Luxembourg. To compensate the farmers of the latter countries, the Common Market would pay them subsidies, lasting through the period of transition, equal to the losses they were suffering through the price change. Mansholt asked that the common grain price be adopted for the 1964–1965 harvests.

Reluctantly, the West German Government declared it could not subscribe to the Mansholt Plan. In plain fact, the West German Farm Federation, apparently distrustful of Common Market compensation, was putting heavy pressure on the government to prevent the lowering of West German grain prices. The French Government also was concerned, lest the raising of French grain prices contribute to inflation within France. Grain-exporting nations outside the Community protested that French farmers, impelled by the hope of greater income, might plant more land to wheat, thus increasing the French grain surplus and choking off imports from abroad.

In the long run, however, it was West German objections that proved decisive. Werner Schwarz, West German agricultural minister, told the Council of Ministers in April 1964 that a common grain price currently was "outside the realm of possibility for us." Already, he said, "an extraordinary unrest has entered the German agricultural sector because of these plans." He did not add, but might have, that the Chris-

Lyndon B. Johnson, then Vice-President of the United States, with Sicco Mansholt, a vice-president of the Common Market Commission. They met in Brussels in November 1963.

tian Democratic Union of West German Chancellor Ludwig Erhard depended heavily on the vote of German farmers to stay in office.

The West German decision was unacceptable to France. December 15, 1964, was set by the French Government as a new deadline for agreement on a common grain price. Otherwise, General de Gaulle indicated, France would "cease to participate" in the Common Market. Faced by this French demand, Professor Erhard's government capitulated.

On December 15, the very day of the deadline, the Six agreed on future grain prices. The soft wheat price, for example, was set at $106 per ton, about $12 a ton less than prevailing West German prices. The Common Market would pay German farmers $300,000,000 in compensation over a three-year period. The West German Government would add a similar amount on its own.

But the Mansholt target of the 1964–1965 harvests had not been met. The new grain prices would come into effect on July 1, 1967. Their over-all effect would be to lower West German grain prices up to 15 per cent and boost French prices by 10 per cent. This would be a boon for French farmers, but not necessarily for the French nation as a whole. French Agriculture Minister Edgard Pisani warned that the French housewife might find herself paying 10 per cent more for her food. None the less, President de Gaulle hailed the grain agreement as opening "all sorts of possibilities in the way of European construction."

This tangled story of agriculture within the Common Market teaches three important lessons. First, it was proving harder to establish a common market for farm products than for industry, where progress was more rapid than the Treaty of Rome originally had foreseen. Second, from time to time during the transition period, problems would arise that might cause a slowdown in one sector or another. In the case of agriculture, West Germany and France had been the nations most directly concerned. In future problems other members of the Six might have the spotlight fall on them.

Third, and perhaps most important, the struggle over agriculture had put the allegiance of the Six to the Common Market to a decisive test. Three times, when dissolution threatened, West Germany had put aside its national interests, at least enough to permit the Community to continue. This augured hopefully for the future. Europeans drew comfort from the fact that the Common Market appeared here to stay, however rocky the future road might be.

Euratom and the "Wise Men"

The European Atomic Energy Community, or Euratom, is the least known of the Community's three institutions, even among Europeans. Unlike the Coal and Steel Community and the Common Market, Euratom does not deal with the products of everyday life, which people buy, sell, or dream about having, like food, clothing, or motorboats. Instead, Euratom works with the atom, still a nebulous concept to most men. Occasionally magazines and newspapers publish pictures of men in white smocks and protective gloves, working at monstrous machines which seem to be "smashing" tiny particles of matter. This, to many people, is Euratom. They do not connect its work with a light switch in their cellar or an electric toaster in the kitchen. Yet the primary objective of Euratom is to supply abundant and cheap electrical power to the peoples of the Six.

From the beginning, Euratom had one advantage over its sister communities. It was entering a new field of endeavor, uncluttered by old economic structures which had to be demolished, before something new could be built. Indeed, as Paul Henri Spaak put it, "the atom and automation are the future."

EURATOM
COMMUNAUTE EUROPEENNE
DE L'ENERGIE ATOMIQUE

EUROPÄISCHE
ATOMGEMEINSCHAFT

COMUNITA' EUROPEA
DELL'ENERGIA ATOMICA

EUROPESE GEMEENSCHAP
VOOR ATOOMENERGIE

L. GIELENS

Euratom headquarters in Brussels; (above) sign at the entrance

The need for concerted action among the Six had been spelled out by "Three Wise Men," who had been appointed to study the atomic capabilities of the Common Market countries at the suggestion of Jean Monnet's Action Committee for a United States of Europe.[1] These three nuclear experts, a Frenchman, a German, and an Italian, presented their report to the governments of the Six, after a tour of atomic installations in the United States, Canada, and Western Europe.

The gist of their findings was that the nations of the Six were far behind the United States, the Soviet Union, and Britain in the development of nuclear energy. The Six faced a long-term shortage of energy which could not be supplied from within, unless they developed their atomic resources. Otherwise they would be obliged to pay billions of dollars annually for imports of coal, oil, and natural gas. Finally, no single country within the Community had the technical or financial resources to tackle nuclear research wholly on its own. All must combine their efforts, or fall hopelessly behind the giants in the field.

The Community's acceptance of this report resulted in the creation of Euratom, which came into being on January 1, 1958, to pool the resources of the Six in the peaceful uses of atomic energy. Euratom would share with the ECSC and the Common Market the Council of Ministers, the European Parliament, and the Court of Justice. Euratom also was authorized to draw on the advice and guidance of the 101-member Economic and Social Committee of the Common Market.

[1] The "Three Wise Men" were Francesco Giordani of Italy, Franz Etzel of West Germany, and Louis Armand, a Frenchman who is credited with originating the name "Euratom."

Like the other two communities, Euratom had its own separate executive Commission, consisting of five men, a smaller body than the nine-member executives of the Common Market and the Coal and Steel Community. Euratom's Commission was to be aided in its work by a special twenty-member Scientific and Technical Committee of nuclear experts from the Six. Also created were a Euratom Supply Agency and a Joint Nuclear Research Center. Like the Common Market, Euratom was headquartered in Brussels.

Experts of the Six forecast that by 1980 the Community would be consuming almost four times as much energy as in 1960. By that time, it was urged, the Six should be producing at least one-quarter of their total electricity needs by atomic means. To attain this goal Euratom adopted a ten-point action program, embracing joint research, the training of young nuclear scientists, and the construction of European nuclear reactors.

By the end of 1963 nuclear power stations in operation in the Community were producing a combined capacity of about 535 megawatts. (A watt is a basic unit of power named after James Watt, a Scotch inventor. A megawatt is one million watts. An ordinary light bulb in the home may consume 60, 100, or as much as 300 watts.) Additional reactors under construction were expected to boost installed nuclear capacity to 2,700 megawatts by 1967. As a measure of the distance yet to go, Euratom hoped to build one hundred nuclear power stations between 1965 and 1980. This would give the Community 40,000 megawatts of nuclear-powered electricity, or about 25 to 30 per cent of the EEC's total estimated needs of electricity in 1980.

Among the Six there were sharply differing levels of nuclear accomplishment, at the time Euratom came into being. France was well in advance, with a small but active nuclear

Nuclear power plant being built at Gundremmingen, West Germany, will produce 237 megawatts of electricity

industry. Then came West Germany and Italy and, far behind, Belgium and the Netherlands. Luxembourg still has no nuclear industry of its own.

Euratom was not intended to absorb these various national programs, but rather to prevent overlapping and repetitive work among the Six through the pooling of research and information. Also, where gaps existed, Euratom could fill in with Community nuclear programs of its own.

To this end Euratom established a $215,000,000 research and development budget for its first five years, 1958–1962.

Nuclear Research Centers at Geel, Belgium; Petten, Holland

For Euratom's next five years, extending through 1967, the Community supplied an additional $425,000,000, with the possibility that this amount would be increased as research expanded. These funds were to be spent in three general ways.

One was the construction of four research centers belonging to the Joint Nuclear Research Center of Euratom. One of these was at Varese-Ispra, north of Milan, Italy; another at Geel, Belgium; a third at Karlsruhe, Germany, and a fourth at Petten, Holland. France already possessed its own nuclear research centers, whose work would be aided by Euratom through "association" contracts.

Apart from establishing its own research centers, Euratom also spent part of its money to assist development projects being conducted by national agencies and private companies throughout the Six. Hundreds of such contracts were signed,

Nuclear Research Center at Varese-Ispra, Italy

involving sometimes a financial grant from Euratom, in other cases the assignment of Euratom teams to work with national groups. A third channel of Euratom investment was the conclusion of nuclear research agreements with governments outside the Six, principally with the United States, but also with Britain, Canada, Argentina, Brazil, and other powers.

Euratom's own research has concentrated generally on two "families" of nuclear reactors, both of which are designed to produce commercial electric power. The first family includes several types of "converter" reactors, which use either natural or enriched uranium for fuel. Most atomic power installations now in operation throughout the world are based on this "converter" type of reactor, which employs various means of converting the energy locked within the uranium atom into usable power.

This type of reactor has the advantage of being already highly developed. The Six could use converter reactors relatively quickly for the production of electric power, particularly since the Community possesses ample reserves of uranium ore, mainly in France. But this "first-generation" type of reactor has distinct limitations. It converts less than one per cent of the potential energy locked within uranium and it burns up, or consumes, more fissionable material than it produces.

To take care of its most immediate needs, Euratom worked toward the development of converter reactors among the Six. But to have concentrated wholly on these would have left the Community unprepared for the time when converter reactors were outmoded by new developments. Thus Euratom also conducted research on a second family of reactors, called "fast breeders." Essentially a breeder reactor is one which produces more atomic fuel than it consumes. It also has the great advantage of utilizing at least 50 per cent of the fissionable energy contained in uranium, with the result that a breeder reactor produces, from a given amount of fuel, one hundred or more times as much power as a converter reactor is able to do.

Euratom signed association contracts on the development of fast breeder reactors with French, West German, and Italian agencies. Seventy-three million dollars were allocated to this program by Euratom during its second five-year period. But breeder reactors require either enriched uranium or plutonium as fuel, beyond the present capacity of the Six to produce. It was at this point that Euratom turned to the United States.

The first agreement between Euratom and the United States Atomic Energy Commission was signed in November 1958. This contract has since been amended frequently to broaden the base of nuclear co-operation. The original agreement established a Joint Power Reactor Program and a Joint Research and Development Program to last for ten years, divided into two five-year periods. During the first five years each side spent about twenty-two and a half million dollars on research, whose results were shared by the United States and Euratom. The general aim of this initial joint research was to lower the costs of electric power production in two types of converter reactors.

Apart from this, the United States also agreed to sell or lease to Euratom enriched uranium and plutonium to be used as fuel in fast breeder reactors. (Uranium in its natural state contains 99.3 per cent of Uranium 238 and approximately seven-tenths of one per cent of Uranium 235. Normally only the latter is fissionable. "Enriched uranium" is uranium that has been processed to increase the percentage of U-235. "Fully enriched" uranium generally contains over 90 per cent of U-235. Plutonium is a man-made chemical element used as reactor fuel which is derived by neutron bombardment of Uranium 238.)

In the spring of 1964 the United States undertook to sell to Euratom 350 kilograms of plutonium. A kilogram is a measure of weight slightly heavier than 2.2 pounds. Sale price of this plutonium was $43 per gram, or $15,050,000 for the total amount. Half of the plutonium involved was destined for fast breeder reactor work at Cadarache, France, and the other half for similar development work at Karlsruhe, West Germany. About the same time Euratom contracted to buy 45 kilograms of plutonium from Great Britain, to be used at Cadarache. This supplemented an earlier purchase of 45 kilograms from Britain, also used at Cadarache.

A second part of the 1964 agreement between the United States and Euratom provided for the lease, or rent, to the

Community of 1700 kilograms of enriched uranium for fast breeder reactor development. The enrichments of this uranium varied from 20 per cent to 60 per cent of U-235. Euratom was to pay the United States about $18,000,000 for the use of this enriched uranium until June 1968. (Enriched uranium of this type is not completely consumed, or lost, by the uses to which it will be put by Euratom. The amount of enriched uranium which will remain after its use by Euratom, will be reprocessed for further service.)

Under a separate agreement signed in Washington May 14, 1964, Euratom agreed to participate with American agencies in the construction of an experimental fast breeder reactor near Fayetteville, Arkansas. This marked the first direct investment of Euratom funds in a project being built in the United States. Under earlier co-operation agreements, the United States and Euratom had spent their research funds on their own sides of the Atlantic and then had pooled their information.

Total cost of the Fayetteville reactor was estimated at $12,350,000. Five million dollars of this was to be provided by the Karlsruhe Research Center of the West German Government, with Euratom contributing 40 per cent of this amount. Another $5,900,000 of the construction costs would be paid by seventeen private American utility companies, banded together as the Southwest Atomic Energy Associates. The remaining construction costs would be borne by the General Electric Company. The role of the United States Atomic Energy Commission was to provide up to $12,700,000 to help the other partners design and operate the reactor. Called SEFOR (Southwest Experimental Fast Oxide Reactor), the project was expected to be completed in 1967.

These various agreements show that co-operation between Euratom and the United States is somewhat different from the relationship existing between the United States and Euratom's sister communities, the Common Market and the Coal and Steel Community. To some extent these latter bodies compete with the United States in world markets. American exports run up against the common external tariff being erected by the Six. But in the field of the atom the imbalance between the United States and Europe still is great. The Six, through Euratom, need and pay for American nuclear help.

Euratom's research work is not confined to the two principal families of reactors described above. It participates with Britain and other European powers in the development at Winfrith, England, of an experimental high-temperature gas reactor, known as the DRAGON project. Euratom also is exploring the possibility of harnessing for peace the awesome power of thermonuclear fusion, so far used only for weapons.

Nuclear fission, or the splitting of the nuclei of atoms, produced the atomic bomb. Fission also is the system employed in converter and breeder reactors. In the case of the reactors the fission process is "controlled," or slowed down. Nuclear fusion, by contrast, involves the merging, or joining, of two light nuclei into a nucleus of heavier mass. The weight of the heavier nucleus is slightly less than the combined weight of the two light nuclei. This slight difference represents the energy released. The fusion process was the basis of the hydrogen bomb. So far scientists have not learned how to "control," or slow down, the fusion process for peaceful uses.

Euratom sends teams of inspectors to its installations and to the plants of its contractors to insure that all fissionable materials owned by Euratom are used strictly as intended— that is, for peaceful purposes and for the specific projects authorized by the Commission. Where American materials are concerned, this security control is supplemented by the sending to Europe of United States experts, who weigh and otherwise check on the use being made of uranium and plutonium sold or leased by the United States Government.

The role of France within Euratom has been predominant, stemming from the nuclear head start France enjoyed at the time the Community came into being. The Euratom Supply Agency noted, for example, that between 1963 and 1967 the Community would need an estimated 7,772 tons of nuclear fuel. Of this total France alone would absorb 7,400 tons.

In another sense the nuclear role of France is unique within the Community. France is the only member of the Six engaged in building its own nuclear military force. Already the French Air Force is equipped with a relatively few atomic bombs. By the early 1970's the French Government plans to have a full range of nuclear-tipped land-based missiles and at least three nuclear-powered submarines, armed with Polaris-type missiles. With no help from the outside, France is building a gaseous diffusion plant, designed to produce enriched uranium, at Pierrelatte in southeastern France, and a hydrogen bomb testing site on the islands of French Polynesia in the South Pacific. The Pierrelatte plant alone will have cost at least one billion dollars by the time it is finished in 1968. The French Government expects to pour eight billion dollars into its nuclear force by 1972, immensely more than it will contribute to Euratom.

This military program is completely separate from Euratom, which concerns itself only with the peaceful uses of atomic energy. The French "force de frappe," or nuclear striking force, is a wholly national endeavor. President de Gaulle has refused to integrate his country's nuclear force within NATO. This attitude is deplored by France's partners among the Six, all of whom have pledged to pool their nuclear defense efforts through NATO.

Within the scope of Euratom, in other words, France is co-operative. But outside Euratom, in the military employment of the atom, General de Gaulle's strong grain of nationalism shows through.

De Gaulle and Nationalism

Caesar may have found all Gaul in three parts divided, but the voice of Gaul today is single. It belongs to President de Gaulle, who strides France like a colossus. De Gaulle's conception of the role of France in the world is almost mystic. "All my life," he wrote in the first volume of his war memoirs, "I have thought of France in a certain way ... The emotional side of me tends to imagine France, like the princess in the fairy stories or the Madonna in the frescoes, as dedicated to an exalted and exceptional destiny. Instinctively I have the feeling that Providence has created her either for complete successes or for exemplary misfortunes. If, in spite of this, mediocrity shows in her acts and deeds, it strikes me as an absurd anomaly, to be imputed to the faults of Frenchmen, not to the genius of the land. But the positive side of my mind also assures me that France is not really herself unless she is in the front rank; that only vast enterprises are capable of counterbalancing the ferments of disintegration inherent in her people; that our country, as it is, surrounded by the others, as they are, must aim high and hold itself straight, on pain of mortal danger. In short, to my mind, France cannot be France without greatness."[1]

This conviction has colored the attitude of General de Gaulle toward the United States, toward Britain, and toward the Common Market. It has made him an object of controversy within the alliance, even as men admired the greatness of his character and his achievements. Twice de Gaulle saved France from the kind of disintegration to which he alluded in his memoirs. The first time was in 1940, when, in the moment of his country's defeat by the Germans, he flew to London and rallied the French people to resistance. He emerged from World War II the undisputed leader of France, though he voluntarily retired from power in 1946, having, in his own words, failed to unify the people of France around him politically.

The second time de Gaulle saved France was in 1958, when the nation was hopelessly mired in a long guerrilla war against Moslem rebels in Algeria. Nearly one million white settlers in Algeria were threatening a reign of terror, if France withdrew from the huge North African territory it had ruled since 1830. Half a million French troops could not pacify the country. Yet the officer corps of the French Army, embittered and humiliated by the French collapse in World War II, by the loss of Lebanon and Syria, the defeat in Indo-China, and the withdrawal from Tunisia and Morocco, was determined to fight on in Algeria and win its first military victory in nearly twenty years.

In this dark hour de Gaulle emerged from retirement at the demand of the nation and again became Premier, later President, of France. He never won the allegiance of the

[1]*The War Memoirs of Charles de Gaulle: The Call to Honor 1940–1942* (New York: Simon and Schuster, 1958).

General Charles de Gaulle is elected President of France.
The ceremony is at the Elysée Palace in Paris.

"pieds noirs," or black feet, as the French settlers in Algeria were called. These latter launched a campaign of murders and bombings, both in Algeria and France, to back up their demand that Algeria remain French. But gradually the great wartime leader persuaded the French people and, equally important, key officers of the French Army that to hold on in Algeria would only bleed France white. With the people of France behind him, de Gaulle in July 1962 brought to a close the last of France's great colonial struggles. Today relations between France and independent Algeria remain relatively friendly, based on the continuing cultural and economic orientation of Algerians toward France.

With these outstanding achievements to his credit, de

Gaulle then added a third triumph. He sealed by referendum the ascendancy of the French President over parliament and obtained a striking electoral success in November 1962, becoming the first French leader in this century to gain a stable majority in the National Assembly. Thus he banished, temporarily at least, the instability of the multiparty system which had hampered French government for many years.

De Gaulle's hands then were freed for what he regarded as his next great task—the reassertion of French influence in Europe. It was the way he went about this that brought him into conflict with the United States and with his partners among the Six. Western Europe, in de Gaulle's view, had not truly gained its postwar independence, for its defense remained dominated by the United States through the military structure of NATO. This structure was in the form of a unified command, within which each of the fifteen members assigned to international control the bulk of its armed forces.

The role of the United States within this system particularly disturbed de Gaulle. Every supreme commander of NATO, beginning with General Eisenhower, had been American. Even more important, the United States was the atomic giant of the alliance. Through NATO, the United States had extended its nuclear shield to cover and protect Western Europe. French, German, Greek, Italian, and other Allied troops had been trained in the use of American nuclear weapons. But only the President of the United States could give the order that would fire those weapons. By law the President retained authority over every nuclear warhead manufactured by the United States, wherever in the world those warheads might be based. This gave the United States monopoly control over NATO's nuclear arsenal, a monopoly which still exists, except for those relatively few nuclear weapons produced by Great Britain.

De Gaulle agreed with other Allied leaders that in the early years after World War II this system had been unavoidable. Without a massive American involvement in Europe, expressed economically through the Marshall Plan and militarily through NATO, the nations of Western Europe could not have recovered and might have slipped behind the Iron Curtain.

But de Gaulle contended that circumstances had changed radically since 1949, when NATO was founded. Western Europe had regained its equilibrium. The developing Common Market was moving the Six toward economic equality with the United States. In these circumstances, the NATO system must be revised to fit the times. Western Europe must gain its nuclear freedom of the United States, just as earlier it had gained its economic independence.

Every President of the United States since Harry Truman had pledged that the United States would defend Europe as it would its own soil. De Gaulle did not doubt this pledge, which had been the foundation of the NATO compact. But, asked de Gaulle, how could Europeans be sure that some future President of the United States might not withdraw American troops from Europe? How could one know "if, when, where, how, and why" the United States would use its nuclear weapons in the event Western Europe were attacked? Was it not possible, he asked, that the United States and the Soviet Union, faced with the prospect of mutual annihilation, might decide not to destroy each other's cities, even if war broke out in Europe?

To guard against such possibilities, de Gaulle declared, Europe must possess its own nuclear weapons, under European command. Otherwise European governments would continue to abdicate a vital part of their responsibility, even of their sovereignty, to a foreign president, sitting in Washington. France would begin by building its own nuclear force, completely under French control. But this in itself would not be enough. The integrated command system of NATO must be abolished, allowing Europeans to create their own separate command, which would co-operate with the United States on a basis of equality.

As steps toward this goal, President de Gaulle began withdrawing French forces from NATO command. He refused to allow the stockpiling of American nuclear warheads on French soil, since he could not control their use. He reduced French Army divisions assigned to NATO from four to two. He withdrew from integrated command French naval units in the Mediterranean and Atlantic. And he began the laborious construction of a French nuclear force.

President Kennedy's Administration, and that of President Johnson after him, agreed that Europe had come far since 1949 and deserved a voice in its own nuclear defense. To this end the United States Government offered to work with its NATO allies toward some form of shared nuclear control. But American leaders were fundamentally opposed to splitting up free world defense into separate American and European commands.

Together, they argued, the United States and Western Europe would always be stronger than the combined weight of the Sino-Soviet bloc. To separate the commands would increase the danger that nuclear war might be triggered off by someone unable to finish the job. The answer, as American officials saw it, was to maintain an indivisible free world defense. The United States would provide the nuclear shield. America and its allies together must furnish the conventional forces—ground troops, based mainly in West Germany— strong enough to hold back a Soviet land attack until Russian intentions could be probed. This would prevent the premature use of nuclear weapons, which might destroy everyone concerned. Furthermore, only the United States could afford to build an adequate nuclear force and keep it up-to-date, matching the Soviet Union in weapons advance. The United States demonstrated with facts and figures that the American nuclear arsenal was overwhelmingly able to defend the entire free world and was too expensive for a nation like France to contemplate.

The logic of this reasoning was accepted by every member of NATO except France. But de Gaulle seemed impervious to the American point of view. To him, this spelled an Atlantic partnership in which Western Europe, including France, would remain a junior partner, and in which nuclear sovereignty would belong to the United States alone.

De Gaulle acknowledged that the United States was a superpower, by virtue of its happy combination of geography, resources, and inventive population. But this was subtly different from saying that the United States was a "great nation." To de Gaulle a nation was made great by reason of its accumulated history, made up in parts of military glory, the conquest and rule of empire, and civilizing mission, including the contribution of language, institutions, and the arts. This was a measure of greatness whose end results were experience and wisdom and whose patina glowed more richly with the passage of time. France, for example, had lost its empire. Yet millions of men—black, yellow, and white, many of whom never had seen France—still spoke French, as a result of the French civilizing mission throughout the world. To de Gaulle, France conformed superbly to his own definition of greatness. So did Britain. But the United States did not. Its status as superpower did not qualify the United States (the "daughter of Europe," in General de Gaulle's phrase) to guide forever the destiny of the free world.

Judges of the European Court of Justice

De Gaulle's sense of nationalism was illustrated by a memorandum which he sent to President Eisenhower on September 17, 1958. In that letter the French leader proposed a kind of three-power directorate, to consist of the United States, Britain, and France, to decide on common policies in Asia, Africa, and elsewhere outside the area already covered by NATO. Each of the three powers would have a veto over the actions of the others. In other words, Washington, Paris, and London would decide unanimously on major policy decisions throughout the world. Except in self-defense, the United States could not use its own nuclear weapons, unless Britain and France approved. France, as a non-nuclear power, was seeking a veto over American nuclear weapons on the grounds that their use inevitably would involve French security. General de Gaulle warned that his future co-operation within NATO depended on the acceptance of his proposal—that is, on the acceptance of France as an equal partner with the United States and Britain in deciding the affairs of the free world.

President Eisenhower, in his reply, recognized that French security would be affected by the explosion of American nuclear weapons. But the security of all other members of NATO would be similarly affected. And the alliance had been built on the principle of an equal voice for all. He suggested, therefore, a system of broader consultation among all fifteen members of NATO, to decide policy on problems lying outside the alliance area.

Essentially, de Gaulle's proposal had been a reassertion of French national interests, or "grandeur," as the General preferred to put it. De Gaulle might resent being left out of what he considered a special relationship between Washington and London. Yet his proposal for a three-power directorate would have left out the other NATO allies, including West Germany and Italy, roughly the equal of France in size and power.

A long series of discussions between American and French officials failed to reconcile the opposing points of view. From that time on de Gaulle co-operated less and less within NATO, turning his attention increasingly to building a strictly European partnership, under the leadership of France. In the nuclear age, he concluded, only nations with nuclear forces could make their voices heard. France would have such a force and its possession, the first among the Six, would help to perpetuate French leadership on the Continent.

In de Gaulle's view, this policy did not make him a bad ally. On the contrary, he insisted that an eventual European nuclear command would co-operate fully with the United

States in targeting and strategy. During the Cuban missile crisis of 1962, when President Kennedy told the Soviets to take their rockets out of Cuba, de Gaulle was one of the first allies to support the United States publicly.

De Gaulle's separatist policy within NATO is the natural outcome of his conviction that alliances are temporary, while nation-states remain. In World War II, Germany, Italy, and Japan had been the enemies. Now all three were members of the free world community and the Soviet Union, an ally during the war, had become the "enemy." Alliances among governments were fluid, but, as de Gaulle saw it, nation-states and their national interests remained constant.

De Gaulle's preoccupation with the role of France carried over into his relations with the Common Market. Prior to the signing of the Treaty of Rome, he had been opposed to the Common Market as an infringement upon the sovereignty of France. Had he been in power during that period, it is possible the Common Market would not have come into being. But de Gaulle had been in retirement when the Treaty of Rome was signed. When he returned to power in 1958, the French leader found France committed to the Common Market. He honored this commitment. Wherever he found institutions in place, he did not tinker. Instead, he erected a roadblock against the political union of the Six, which had not yet been "institutionalized," or achieved. That is, the kind of unity he proposed was unacceptable to the others.

Foreseeing the inevitability of some kind of union, de Gaulle pressed for a loose federation of sovereign national states, a "Europe of fatherlands," in which an intergovernmental council would seek to co-ordinate European policy. Within this federation each government would retain veto power. He proposed that the economic commissions of the Common Market be supplemented by "a political commis-

sion, a defense commission, and a cultural commission."
These commissions would study relevant questions and present their conclusions to periodic meetings of the chiefs of state or heads of government, who then would take decisions which would be the "decisions of Europe." Europe, the French President contended, would be able to "have no living reality if it did not consist of France with its Frenchmen, Germany with its Germans, Italy with its Italians, etc." At the present time only those entities known as national states could furnish Europe with the needed elements of "action, authority, and responsibility."

This proposal for a loose association of fully sovereign states, each equipped with a veto, was opposed vigorously by the rest of the Six. The whole tenor of the Treaty of Rome, as they saw it, impelled the Six toward a supranational union —that is, "above nationality"—in which each member would cede some sovereignty to a central body, as already was being done in the economic field.

The other five unanimously opposed de Gaulle's separatist tactics within NATO. They all favored the closest possible integration with the United States in the defense field. They were suspicious, therefore, of de Gaulle's suggestion that the Six establish a committee of their defense ministers—a kind of inner group within NATO. They saw this as an attempt by the French leader to use the Community as an instrument of French national policy. They insisted that their defense responsibilities were adequately expressed through NATO.

Also troubling to the Six was de Gaulle's suggestion that his proposed political council of heads of government should have a role in the economic field. His spokesmen did not define what this role should be, but the other five suspected de Gaulle was seeking to cast an arm of national control over the operations of the existing treaties and their institutions.

To this, all five were opposed. De Gaulle's concepts, presented as a draft treaty for political union, were rejected by the rest of the Six.

Belgium and the Netherlands in particular wanted a supranational union, in which voting would be by weighted majority, as was the practice within the Common Market. Without some cession of sovereignty by all, these two small nations foresaw themselves, along with Luxembourg, being submerged by the weight of the big three, France, West Germany, and Italy. In the kind of Europe advanced by de Gaulle, the Dutch and Belgians feared the voice of the small powers would be overwhelmed. To protect themselves from the uncertainties of French and German politics, Belgium and Holland pressed for the entry of Britain into the Common Market. Britain, traditionally friendly to the Low Countries, would act as a stable counterweight to France and West Germany.

De Gaulle's abrupt exclusion of Britain in January 1963 threw the Common Market into turmoil. All members except France had wanted Britain in. West Germany, particularly under its new chancellor, Professor Ludwig Erhard, continued to support the eventual entry of Britain. So did Italy. Belgium and Holland went further. They said they would not discuss political union until Britain had become a member of the Common Market. Later they modified this ban on discussions, but insisted no decision on political union could be reached until the position of Britain had been made clear.

Essentially this impasse between France and its partners remains. On defense and political philosophy the five stand against one. Superficially, this resembles the time in 1954 when the French National Assembly killed the proposal for a European Army. De Gaulle, like the National Assembly of 1954, appears to have stymied progress toward political union.

So he has, but there is an important distinction to be made. The existing institutions of the Common Market have gone right on functioning, despite de Gaulle's veto of the British. Moreover, the economy of France continues to improve and to depend more and more upon the success of the Common Market. Increasingly, French industrialists are adapting their operations to the giant market of the Six. French farmers need the Community as an outlet for their crops. A common market in agriculture, one of the chief achievements of the Community, was agreed upon after, not before, de Gaulle had excluded the British. Bit by bit, as in the warning system

Heavy industry in France. A turboalternator is mounted.

Automobile factory outside Paris

set up against inflation, the Common Market has been broadening its supranational character, despite General de Gaulle.

Progress may be slow, slower than the other partners want. But the Common Market appears to have grown beyond de Gaulle's ability to halt it, even if he wished. The livelihood of too many Frenchmen depends on the success of the great experiment. In this sense the Common Market has become a part of the national interests of France, which President de Gaulle so zealously guards.

Proof of the pudding came on April 16, 1964, when de Gaulle made a radio and television address to his people. In that address he spoke of French farmers and of the fact that the European Economic Community was opening "to their production, to their sales, to their profits, vast new perspectives." Later in his talk he described the Common Market as "little by little becoming essential to our (French) prosperity." This was the language of a man who had accepted the Common Market as here to stay.

Britain and the Veto

On the afternoon of January 14, 1963, hundreds of reporters from many countries sat on spindly gilt chairs in a glittering chamber of the Elysée Palace in Paris. At the front of the huge room sat the entire French Government, headed by Premier Georges Pompidou. Television lights mounted near the ceiling poured down a hot blue-white glare. Precisely at three o'clock red velvet curtains parted and the audience hushed. Into the room stepped the tall commanding figure of General de Gaulle. Everyone in the room rose in respect, as the President of France approached a giant gold-painted chair standing on a dais. De Gaulle bowed slightly and sat down. It was the eighth press conference he had held since his return to power in 1958. He was about to drop a bomb-shell, cloaked in elegant French, but a bombshell none the less, whose reverberations would echo around the world.

In October 1961 Britain had applied to join the Common Market. Since that time negotiations had been going on in Brussels, between Britain on the one hand and the Six on the other. Encouraged by the British example, Denmark, Nor-way, and the Republic of Ireland had applied for full membership. Indeed, Ireland's application had been filed ahead of that of Britain. But Britain was the key, and the eyes of the free world hung on the negotiations under way in Brussels. The entry of Britain, with its special trading links throughout the world and its status as a major power, would have magnified greatly the scope of the EEC.

By January 1963 British and European negotiators had solved many difficult problems. Others remained, but to the Common Market Commission and to five members of the Six, the stage seemed set for British entry and the enlargement of the EEC.

Then de Gaulle spoke in Paris. Britain, he asserted, had shown herself unready for membership in the Common Market. The Treaty of Rome, the President continued, had been based on the "solidarity" of six Continental powers—France, West Germany, Italy, Belgium, the Netherlands, and Luxembourg—which had similar economies, working conditions, and outlooks. Britain, by contrast, de Gaulle said, had an "insular" and "maritime" economy, based on the importation of "cheap" foodstuffs from North and South America and from the Commonwealth. (The Commonwealth is a world-wide grouping of nations, comprising Britain and most of her former colonies and dependencies in North America, Africa, and Asia. The Commonwealth is today's looser counterpart of the former British Empire.)

Such a Britain in no way could fit into the Common Market mold, de Gaulle declared, unless it agreed to drop its special economic ties with the Commonwealth and its special defense ties with the United States. French Government spokesmen, later explaining the President's decision, noted that just before de Gaulle's press conference, Britain had accepted an American offer to buy Polaris missiles from the United States, on the condition that these missiles and their British submarines would be assigned to NATO. To de Gaulle, this meant that Britain had signed away its nuclear independence.

French sources also affirmed that in December 1962 de Gaulle had asked British Prime Minister Harold Macmillan whether the latter's government was prepared to make all necessary adjustments to join the Common Market. Macmillan had replied in the affirmative, the French sources said, but had—from de Gaulle's point of view—qualified his response by stressing the importance of Britain's ties with the Commonwealth. This had been followed up by Mr. Macmillan's acceptance of the Polaris missile offer from the United States. (President Kennedy had extended the same offer to France. De Gaulle had declined it as incompatible with French nuclear independence.)

It was then, according to French officials, that de Gaulle had made up his mind finally that Britain was not ready to join the Common Market. To have accepted such a Britain, de Gaulle declared at his press conference, would have obliged the Six to accept other European countries, also knocking on the door. This would have diluted the EEC within a "colossal Atlantic community," which inevitably would have been dominated by the United States. This would have transformed the Common Market into something which France had not wanted when it signed the Treaty of Rome. The policy of France was to build a Europe dependent upon itself in the realms of foreign policy, economy, defense, and culture; a Europe that would not be drowned in an Atlantic sea and thereby lose its true personality. The French Government, therefore, would exercise its veto power to end the negotiations going on with the British in Brussels.

This decision struck the Six like a thunderclap. In vain Jean Monnet recalled that the British, when they had applied for membership, had "renounced all preference in regard to the Commonwealth" and had agreed to accept the Treaty of Rome without reservations. In vain Walter Hallstein, president of the Common Market Commission, pointed out that progress made to date in the negotiations promised a reasonable chance of final success.

These arguments fell on deaf ears. De Gaulle's complaint was more fundamental. He appeared to regard Britain's entry as a wedge which the United States would use to manipulate the affairs of the Six and to widen American influence in Europe. Already the United States dominated European defense through NATO. A Common Market including Britain would offer another channel of penetration to the United States. The first task of the Six was to gain full control over their own destiny, including nuclear defense. Then the Six would be in a position to consider British membership—if Britain meanwhile had shorn itself of special ties to the United States and to the Commonwealth. That day had not arrived.

On January 29, 1963, the negotiations with Britain were broken off. The applications of Denmark, Norway, and Ireland were quietly shelved. The EEC remained a club of Six, as it is today. All five partners of France deplored the exclusion of Britain. Belgium and Holland saw the loss of a great power traditionally friendly to them. The West Germans sensed the French were seeking to isolate West Germany from Britain and the United States. This pressure the Germans rejected. The British also were among West Germany's best customers.

On the "technocrat" side, leaders of the ECSC and Euratom Commissions joined Professor Hallstein in criticizing the French move. Britain's membership, according to Pietro Malvestiti, president of the High Authority of the Coal and Steel Community, "would have been a source of strength to

Europe." E.M.J.A. Sassen, a member of the Euratom Commission, declared that British membership in Euratom would have represented "a massive increase in the atomic potential of an integrated Europe." "The Communities," he said, "are above all *European* Communities, and that is not synonymous with *continental*."

In February the European Parliament, meeting in Strasbourg, summed up the general feeling by passing unanimously the following resolution, with Gaullist deputies abstaining:

The Parliament:
Stresses that the final aim of European integration is the creation of a United States of Europe, a supranational economic and political Community based on equality of rights for member countries and possessing its own institutions independent of member Governments;

*The British delegation at the end of fruitless
negotiations between Britain and the Six*

Believes that only such a Europe, within an Atlantic Partnership and in equality with the United States, will be able to fulfill the role which is required of it for the defense of the free world and for the maintenance of peace and general economic progress;

Recalls that in a number of resolutions the Parliament has supported British membership and that of other countries, providing that such membership does not compromise the process of integration and that the Treaties of Rome (Common Market and Euratom) and Paris (ECSC) are not endangered . . .

Expresses its grave concern at the unilateral rupture of the negotiations between the Six and the British Government, and asks the Council of Ministers to insure that the conference responsible for examining the problems of accession holds regular meetings, so that the entry of new members, particularly the United Kingdom (Britain), may be facilitated . . .

This resolution was approved by non-Gaullist French deputies to the European Parliament. Everyone but the

The European Parliament meeting in Strasbourg, February 1963

Gaullists, in other words, wanted Britain in the club. The British played too important a role in the affairs of Europe, politically, militarily, and economically, to be left out. At the end of the long negotiations Edward Heath, leader of the British delegation, declared: "We shall not turn our backs on the continent." Professor Hallstein replied: "And we shall not turn our backs on England."

But all sides recognized that, so long as de Gaulle remained President of France, the chances of British entry were slim. The best the five partners could wring from the French Government was an agreement that contacts with Britain would be kept up through the medium of the Western European Union, the seven-nation group that had been organized after the defeat of the European Army proposal in 1954.

Maurice Couve de Murville, a Protestant intellectual who was de Gaulle's trusted foreign minister, stressed that Britain could join the Common Market, as soon as it chose "Europe" over the Commonwealth and the United States. Meanwhile, the Common Market would go on as before. Hallstein warned that the blow of the veto must not be allowed to jeopardize the Community itself.

The Common Market, he affirmed, is more than "a particular form of co-operation between sovereign governments . . . It has its own personality. In accordance with a carefully worked out constitution this personality speaks and acts through the institutions. These organs act in their own right. Participation is not a matter of choice for those concerned, but is their first duty and stems from the fact that they belong to the Community." These institutions must continue to function in a normal way, however much the members regretted President de Gaulle's veto of the British.

Gradually the Common Market recovered its momentum. Important decisions were taken, including general agreement on agriculture and the establishment of an anti-inflation program. Politically, however, the Community had run up against a roadblock that seemed for the moment to be insurmountable. This meant two things. First, the Community was not likely to expand its membership significantly until the British problem had been solved. Second, the Six might not progress toward real political union among themselves until Britain had become a member.

Because of this, it is important to understand why the negotiations at Brussels had been so difficult, quite apart from de Gaulle. For centuries Great Britain had stayed aloof from permanent entanglement on the European Continent. She had played the role of balance of power. Britain's historic aim had been to prevent any single European power from becoming strong enough to dominate Europe and thereby threaten the independence of Great Britain. To this end the British had thrown their weight on the side of weaker, threatened powers, including often Belgium and Holland.

This diplomatic freedom of movement was enhanced by the existence of the English Channel, which made difficult the invasion of Britain. England's position as an island had other results. It caused the British to seek to control the seas, as protection for the imports of food and raw materials which the British Isles vitally needed. Mastery of the seas opened up vast colonizing and commercial enterprises far away from Europe. Finally, there was in the British people a strong conviction of nationalism, of being "different" from the peoples on the Continent.

These factors continued to play a role in British thinking even after World War II. Added to them was the new fact of Britain's special relationship with the United States, now the most powerful nation in the world. To many Englishmen this partnership, and the remaining links with the Commonwealth, took precedence over Europe.

Against this background the British Government had disappointed Jean Monnet by declining to join the Coal and Steel Community and, later, the proposed European Defense Community. In neither case was there outright refusal by the British. Rather there were counter proposals from London that would have diluted the concepts of the Six, intent on building a new society with supranational overtones. This possibility of loss of sovereignty troubled British leaders, both Conservative and Labour. In this respect they agreed with General de Gaulle. They were willing to consider co-operation among sovereign governments, but unwilling to tie Britain to the Continent by unbreakable chains. As a result the Six built their Community, step by step, without Britain.

In the "relance," or renewal, that followed the failure of the EDC in 1954, Britain took the lead by proposing the Western European Union as a vehicle for rearming West Germany. This was a notable contribution by the British. But WEU, as we have noted, was a co-operative arrangement among sovereign states, not a step toward union.

Again, at the invitation of the Six, Britain initially took part in the Spaak Committee discussions that led to the Common Market and Euratom. At the end of 1955, however, Britain withdrew from the discussions rather than commit herself politically. In 1956 the British Government advanced the concept of a European Free Trade Area, to include all eighteen members of the Organization for European Economic Co-operation, forerunner of the OECD.

The basic idea behind this Free Trade Area proposal was to give Britain some form of association with the Common Market, without binding the British to the latter's strict requirements. Under the British proposal the eighteen members of the OEEC would have abolished all tariffs on industrial trade among them. But each member would have preserved its own national tariff system vis-à-vis the outside world. There would have been no common external tariff erected by the eighteen, as was the case with the Six. Also, trade in farm products was excluded from Britain's Free Trade Area proposal.

British leaders felt this was as far as they could go. They could not agree to a common external tariff against non-members, since they were committed to accept many Commonwealth exports duty free. Yet without some form of association with the Six, Britain stood to lose rich markets on the Continent. Within the Six, many European business-men opposed the Free Trade Area. They felt that British industry, bolstered by duty-free raw material and food imports from the Commonwealth, would be given a competitive advantage. For the same reason some political leaders among the Six felt Britain was trying to have its cake and eat it, too, by gaining the benefits of tariff-cutting without making the sacrifices required of Common Market members. These leaders opposed membership of the Six in a larger, looser community, at least until the Common Market had had time to prove itself.

It fell to General de Gaulle, following his return to power in 1958, to deliver the coup de grâce to the European Free Trade Area. France, his spokesmen said, found the concept incompatible with the road the French Government had chosen to follow within the Common Market. This decision pleased French businessmen and bankers and was in general accord with Common Market thinking. Observers noted also that de Gaulle had made his move, after having been rebuffed by Washington and London in his search for a tripartite directorate of free world affairs.

Collapse of the free trade plan left Britain and some other European countries in an increasingly awkward situation. The Common Market was proving successful, so much so that Greece and Turkey were seeking association with it. There seemed danger that European trade would become more and more polarized on the Six. To protect themselves, Britain and six other members of the OEEC banded together in a European Free Trade Association (EFTA). Its members were Britain, Denmark, Norway, Sweden, Austria, Switzerland, and Portugal. These seven pledged to cut their internal tariffs progressively to zero, until they had achieved a free trade area among themselves. But there would be no common external tariff. Each member would determine its own tariff structure with the outside world. Thus Britain's Commonwealth preference system would remain intact.

EFTA was founded in January 1960 and set up its headquarters in Geneva. To journalists, the members of the European Free Trade Association became known as the "Outer Seven," while the Common Market was labeled the "Inner Six." Europe, it was said, was now at Sixes and Sevens.

On paper EFTA was reasonably impressive, with a population of ninety million persons. But of this total Britain alone had fifty-one millions, leaving only thirty-nine million persons for the other six combined. This meant that British exports could expand relatively little within the limited EFTA market. Sweden and Switzerland had their own manufactured products to sell, while Danish farm exports competed with British and duty-free Commonwealth foodstuffs within the British market. It soon became apparent that EFTA was no true rival of the Common Market, in the sense of bringing trade benefits to its members.

British businessmen looked hungrily across the Channel at the growing market among the Six. French and German manufacturers were benefiting from the elimination of internal duties, while British exports would be butting against the common external tariff of the Six. On the political side,

Britain's diplomatic influence threatened to shrink in a world of giants—the United States, the Soviet Union, and the expanding Common Market, whose end goal was political union. The conviction widened among British Government leaders that Britain had been mistaken not to join the European unity movement in the beginning.

On July 31, 1961, Prime Minister Macmillan told the House of Commons that Britain, in effect, was ready to turn its back on centuries of tradition. The British Government would seek membership in the Common Market, if mutually acceptable conditions could be found. This last was the key, for Britain brought three enormously difficult problems to the negotiations which opened with the Six in Brussels that October.

1. *EFTA.* Britain had promised it would not desert its Outer Seven partners by joining the Common Market, unless all other EFTA members also reached some form of accommodation with the Six. This is what General de Gaulle later meant when he declared in January 1963 that the entry of Britain would have brought in other nations whose membership would have diluted the EEC.

Apart from economic considerations, three members of EFTA—Sweden, Austria, and Switzerland—were committed to neutrality between East and West in the Cold War. They could not accept political union with the Six, all of whom were members of NATO. But all members of the Common Market agreed that the Treaty of Rome should not be watered down. An applicant must hew to the full line of the treaty's requirements or remain outside.

2. *The Commonwealth.* Under a long-established trade preference system, Britain accepted many Commonwealth exports at low or zero tariffs. This system would have had to end if Britain joined the Common Market. The EEC's common external tariff would go up around Britain, forcing

Sheep-raising is vital to New Zealand's economy

exports from the Commonwealth to jump a wall to get inside their old British market. This possibility brought strong cries of protest from Commonwealth sources.

New Zealand, which sold almost all its exports of lamb and mutton, cheese and butter to Great Britain, would have been hardest hit. Nigeria, too, sold almost half its exports to the United Kingdom. In varying degree the economies of Canada, Australia, and other Commonwealth partners would have had to adjust to the shock of Britain's entry into the Common Market.

But there was another side to this coin. Just after World War II the Commonwealth had been Britain's biggest customer, buying nearly 60 per cent of all British exports. During this early postwar period only 25 per cent of British sales went to Western Europe. As Commonwealth countries developed their economies and sought new trading outlets, they also varied their sources of supply. To obtain new markets in Japan, for example, Australia agreed to buy more Japanese manufactures. Such bilateral trade agreements cut into British exports to the Commonwealth.

Simultaneously British businessmen began to expand their sales in Western Europe. In 1962 Europe replaced the Commonwealth as Britain's leading customer. Clearly Britain could not count on the Commonwealth to absorb the exports which the "tight little island" had to sell. The natural British market lay in Western Europe, whose heartland was the Six. Membership in the Common Market would have been a boon to British business.

But ties within the Commonwealth, emotional, political, and economic, tugged strongly at many British hearts. Thus British membership in the EEC must include arrangements to help those Commonwealth members, like New Zealand, whose dependence on the United Kingdom market still was major. For African members of the Commonwealth, the British Government sought an association status similar to that enjoyed by former French and Belgian colonies.

3. *British agriculture.* In the spring of 1964 a British diplomat stationed in Paris made a trip home to London. While there he bought a leg of lamb and took it back to Paris. In England he had paid the equivalent of four dollars for that leg of lamb. In France the same piece of meat would have cost twelve dollars.

This illustrated a general fact. Housewives among the Six paid much more for their food than did housewives in Britain. Food prices were generally low in England, high on the Continent, though there were exceptions to the rule. Only 4 per cent of Britain's population works on the farm. These relatively few farmers produce about half the food needs of the British Isles. The rest must be imported, making Britain the largest single food importer in the world.

Often it costs British farmers more to produce their crops than they can get in the local marketplace, competing against foodstuffs imported at low tariffs or duty free. The government then steps in and pays British farmers cash subsidies. It also pays them to fertilize and lime their land and to modernize their farm equipment. One purpose of this program has been to protect the British people as much as possible against food shortages in wartime, when British ports might be blockaded by enemy submarines.

But this system of cash subsidy would have had to disappear if Britain joined the Common Market. It would be replaced by the internal levy method adopted by the Six, with the levies gradually to disappear until a common price level and free agricultural trade had been achieved by 1970. This price level, established by the competitive operation of supply and demand, would tend to raise food prices in Britain toward the Continental level.

Some British farmers would benefit from this, others would not. But the British housewife almost certainly would pay more for her food. This might cause widespread ramifications, including the demand by British factory workers for higher wages. Higher pay might force British manufacturers to raise their prices, making British products less competitive on the world market. For all these reasons, the question of British agriculture was a touchy one at Brussels.

For fifteen months British negotiators and their Common Market colleagues wrestled with these problems, until General de Gaulle ended it all in January 1963. After the veto, the European Parliament demanded a balance sheet on the negotiations from the Common Market Commission. The latter's survey showed that the problem of absorbing Britain's EFTA partners within a Common Market framework had scarcely been touched. The EFTA question had been postponed until the outcome of the British negotiations became clear.

The record on the Commonwealth was mixed. Arrangements had been agreed upon to cushion the adjustment period for underdeveloped nations of the Commonwealth, in the event of Britain's entry. African and Caribbean Commonwealth members would be offered association with the EEC. The question of industrial imports from Canada, Australia, and New Zealand had been solved. But agreement had not been reached on the more complex problem of agricultural imports from the Commonwealth, including New Zealand's vital dependence on the British market.

Progress had been limited on the task of reconciling British farm practices with those of the Six. But the Commission had sensed, just before the negotiations ended, that the British were prepared to scale down their demands.

"In the light of the above outline," Professor Hallstein told the European Parliament, "the prospects of the conference appeared as follows: it is impossible to consider the negotiations, at the moment when they were interrupted, as having failed in practice. It is equally impossible to say that the negotiations had already to all intents and purposes succeeded . . . It would rather be true to say that they had reached a difficult stage in which the British side, too, would have had to make a number of considerable concessions, but that there was a reasonable chance of reaching agreement . . . There can be no doubt that the chance of success was great enough to justify continuing the negotiations."

In the troubled months following the General's veto, the British economy did not go into a tailspin. On the contrary,

British exports to Common Market countries kept on climbing, especially to France, whose government had excluded Britain from the EEC. This was partly because French external tariffs, traditionally high, were lowering year by year toward the arithmetical average of the final common external tariff. This made British goods a bit less expensive than they had been in France.

With West Germany, Britain's best customer among the Six, the situation was different. German tariffs, traditionally low, were rising toward the arithmetical average, making it more difficult for British goods to compete in the West German market. Furthermore, German and French manufacturers were due to benefit more and more from the reduction of internal Common Market duties, tipping the balance in their favor.

Britain also was selling more goods to its partners in EFTA. In 1961 the British had exported about $100,000,000 worth of goods each month to the other six members of EFTA. By 1963 this had risen to $117,000,000 monthly, aided in part by the reduction of internal tariffs within the European Free Trade Association. This growth was healthy, but it was based on a limited population of 39,000,000 persons. EFTA alone could not answer Britain's need to increase its exports.

Neither could the Commonwealth. In dollar value, Britain sold less to the Commonwealth in 1963 than it had in 1961. By 1963 the Commonwealth was taking only about 25 per cent of all British exports. The pattern showed a steadily declining share of British exports going to the Commonwealth, as the latter—particularly the white nations of the old British Empire—industrialized themselves and tended to become economically more self-sufficient.

All these factors, taken together, continued to impel Britain toward the ideal solution of membership in the

Steel mill in Luxembourg

Common Market, the fastest-growing trading area in the world. By 1963 Britain was selling nearly twice as much to the Six as it was to its partners in EFTA. But only through membership could Britain be assured of a satisfactory share of future Common Market trade. So, at least, it seemed to Conservative Party leaders and to British businessmen generally.

None of these arguments seemed likely to prevail, so long as de Gaulle remained President of France. Britain would stay outside the Common Market and EFTA would go on operating as a separate entity, planning its own development moves. The shape of EFTA might change somewhat. Austria, for example, which did more than half of all its trading with the Six, continued to seek some form of association with the Common Market, even after the British veto. Nor was it certain what long-range attitude the British Labour Party, under Prime Minister Harold Wilson, would adopt toward the EEC.

Eventually, however, the question of British membership almost certainly will revive—a key, not only to Britain's economic future, but to political progress among the Six.

The United States and Europe

From the end of World War II until June 30, 1962, the United
States gave nearly twenty-three billion dollars in economic
and military aid to the six members of the European Economic
Community. Of this huge total, France received the most,
$9,584,000,000. Italy came next, with $5,145,000,000, fol-
lowed by West Germany, which received $4,013,000,000. The
Netherlands was given $2,107,000,000 and Belgium and
Luxembourg together absorbed the rest, $1,891,000,000.

Put in simpler terms, this meant about $127 from every
child, man, and woman in the United States, to the peoples
of the Six. This enormous aid package would not have been
given had the American people not been convinced that the
well-being of the United States depended on the revival of
Western Europe. Without a healthy European community,
there would have been only feeble markets for American
goods. The Soviet Union, with huge armies at hand and no
ocean to cross, would have cast its shadow across Europe to
the coasts of France.

American aid, as we have seen, was extended militarily
through NATO and economically through the Marshall Plan.

The first goal of the Marshall Plan had been the economic reconstruction of Western Europe. But beyond this, American planners had looked toward political unity among the European allies. A small country, it was reasoned, could make little individual contribution to the security of the free world. Joined together, as one American diplomat put it, "the whole would be greater than the sum of its parts." In unity there would be strength.

Central to this thinking was the need to give the German people an opportunity to belong to a strong Western community, instead of being cut adrift between East and West. Young Germans in particular must be shown that they "belonged" to the Western world. But Germany must not be allowed to dominate the future Europe, as had happened so often in the past. The answer seemed to be a closely knit community, embracing as many countries as possible, in which no single power could assert control.

Against this background, it was natural for the United States Government to support the unity efforts of the Six. The Coal and Steel Community, the Common Market, Euratom—all received the warm endorsement of the United States. For the same reason, Washington applauded Britain's decision to knock on the door in Brussels. The adhesion of Britain, it was thought, would strengthen the stability of Europe.

But the United States Government, like the Six themselves, was opposed to any watering down of the Treaty of Rome to accommodate a new member. The essence of the Common Market, its real meaning, was the gradual institution of common economic policies, leading inevitably to some form of political union. Such an integrated Europe, in the American view, had the best chance of remaining strong and viable, immune to outside threats. Thus the United States,

Italian oil refinery workers in Sicily

again like the Six, opposed the entry of the neutrals—Austria, Sweden, and Switzerland—unless they subscribed fully to the Treaty of Rome. To dilute the rules by which the Six operated, merely to accommodate purely economic and trade problems of outside powers, would have been contrary to Europe's long-range interests.

American officials understood and sympathized with the fact that the European neutrals did the bulk of their trading with the Six. The United States also faced the possible loss of traditional markets, as the Six eased their internal trade restrictions and built a wall against the outside world. But trade difficulties must give way before the broad objective of European unity. In the long run a solidly constructed Europe, based on the example of the Common Market, would be beneficial to the entire free world.

This Europe, the United States hoped, would be linked to the United States and Canada in a genuine Atlantic partnership. On July 4, 1962, Independence Day in the United States, President Kennedy proclaimed a new doctrine of "interdependence." He saluted the nations of Western Europe for having buried their old enmities in favor of common efforts

Italian women process peaches

President John F. Kennedy speaks in St. Paul's Church,
Frankfurt, West Germany

to solve their problems. To help them be able to do so, the President recalled, had been an objective of American policy for seventeen years.

Now it was time for a united Europe to join hands with the United States, on a basis of equality. Together, Mr. Kennedy declared, the United States and a united Europe could contribute more importantly to free world defense and could help underdeveloped nations—the peoples of Asia, Africa, and Latin America—to lift themselves out of poverty. The President pledged his government's readiness to adhere to a "declaration of interdependence" and to "discuss with a united Europe the ways and means of forming a concrete Atlantic association."

Speaking in Frankfurt, West Germany, in June 1963—five months before his assassination—President Kennedy further developed this theme. "The future of the West," he said, "lies in Atlantic Partnership—a system of co-operation, interdependence, and harmony—whose peoples can jointly meet their burdens and opportunities throughout the world. Some say that it is only a dream, but I do not agree. A generation of achievement—the Marshall Plan, NATO, the Schuman Plan, and the Common Market—urges us up the path to greater unity."

This was a far cry from the assertion by George Washington, first President of the United States, that Europe had "a set of primary interests, which to us have none, or a very remote relation . . ." For more than 150 years Americans had obeyed Washington's injunction to avoid foreign entanglements. His advice at the time he spoke had been wise, for, until the United States gained its independence, and even after, European wars had caused a backlash of trouble in America.

Former Secretary of State Dean Acheson outlined this history in a speech at The Hague. "Every European war was extended to North America," Mr. Acheson declared, "so much so that they even acquired American names." He then recited a long list of European wars, beginning with the League of Augsburg, or King William's War, to the Napoleonic Wars which had caused fighting in North America in 1812.

Subsequently, Acheson continued, the United States focused its energies on eliminating European sovereignties from the Western Hemisphere, and avoiding involvement in foreign wars. Small wonder that George Washington's advice remained a maxim, right down to the twentieth century and World War I. That war, and its terrible successor less than twenty-five years later, taught Americans that the world indeed had become one; that isolation no longer would suffice to protect the United States. The best way to insure peace, it was seen, was to remain strongly involved in the affairs of Europe, to help give them direction. Hence the Marshall Plan and NATO.

By the time Mr. Kennedy spoke of Atlantic "interdependence," a still further development had taken place. No longer was the United States rich and Europe poor. No longer was all the wealth on one side of the Atlantic. So strong had Western Europe become, and particularly the nations of the Six, that it was now their turn to help the United States. The latter, with world-wide military and foreign aid commitments, was spending more abroad than its trade could earn. It was running a deficit balance of payments.

Americans still were selling more goods (farm products and manufactures) overseas than they were buying. The *balance of trade* was favorable to the United States. But the over-all *balance of payments* includes items other than trade. American tourists were ranging the world, taking millions of dollars with them. American companies were investing heavily in new plant and equipment overseas, particularly inside the Common Market. The United States Government was spending billions of dollars yearly on foreign aid to underdeveloped nations and was maintaining half a million American soldiers in Europe. In 1964 the United States spent more than one million dollars a day in South Vietnam, helping that government fight Communist guerrillas. All these factors put together meant that more gold and dollars were flowing out of the United States than were flowing in.

President Kennedy meant the phrase literally, when he

spoke of the need for Atlantic partnership. Both sides, Europe and America, needed the co-operation of each other to keep their economies in trim. Within the twenty-nation Organization for Economic Co-operation and Development, steps were taken to co-ordinate economic policies across the Atlantic. In particular the United States urged its Allies to increase their share of the foreign aid burden. On the American side, Congress passed the Trade Expansion Act of 1962, giving the President broad authority to cut tariffs up to 50 per cent, in return for reciprocal cuts by other nations. The purpose of this act was to liberalize and increase world trade by removing artificial restrictions wherever possible.

At the heart of the problem for the United States lay its relations with the Six—the countries which the United States had done so much to help. Trade in manufactured goods with the Common Market was not of first concern to the United States. American refrigerators, sewing machines, electronic computers, cameras, and a thousand other items still found a ready market within the EEC. "Made in America" remained a mark of quality in Europe.

Farm products from the United States also sold widely in the EEC. But their future sales appeared threatened and this was what concerned American officials. The United States was the world's largest exporter of farm goods. American wheat farmers depended on foreign markets for more than half of their production. Growers of soybeans, feed grains, tobacco, rice, and other products were heavily dependent on sales overseas. One-fourth of all goods exported by the United States were products grown on farms. Yearly exports of American farm goods amounted to five billion dollars.

Within this total, the European Economic Community was America's largest customer. During the fiscal year from July 1, 1961 to June 30, 1962 the United States sold $1,200,-

000,000 worth of farm products to the EEC. The next year this total dropped by about $125,000,000—because the EEC, having agreed on its common agricultural policy, was beginning to protect its own farmers with variable levies. This system, the reader will recall, allowed governments of the Six to give preference to their own farmers by charging fluctuating import duties on farm goods from outside the EEC. Purpose of the variable levies was to make imported farm goods more expensive than the home-grown product.

The United States watched this process with dismay. Americans heard General de Gaulle declare that the Six should be largely self-sufficient in foodstuffs. The EEC appeared to be closing the door on American farm goods. Slightly more than half of all United States agricultural exports would not be affected by variable levies. These products, including soybeans, raw cotton, canned fruits, and others, were subject to tariffs fixed within the world-wide General Agreement on Tariffs and Trade. On most of these items the EEC could not raise tariffs without giving the United States compensation.

But 48 per cent of the value of all American farm exports to the EEC—just under $500,000,000 worth—was subject to variable levies. On this list were wheat and other grains, by far the largest items of trade. In the fiscal year 1961-1962, for example, the United States sold $409,847,000 worth of grains to the Six. American officials pointed out that in bad crop years Europeans depended on American wheat for their bread. "It just is not possible to say, yes, one wants to make use of this (American) productive capacity in bad years but in good years, one will keep it out." These were the words of John W. Tuthill, United States Ambassador to the EEC. What the United States wanted was continued "reasonable access" to its traditional markets in Europe.

In 1964 the British Government gratified the United States by guaranteeing American grain farmers one-third of future British import needs. The Common Market members refused to sign such a guarantee. For one thing, they had been unable at that time to agree among themselves on a common grain price. Until this was achieved, they could not estimate accurately future levels of grain production within the EEC.

The Community sympathized with American balance of payments difficulties, and with the desire of American farmers to keep their overseas markets. But the EEC had its own balance of trade problem with the United States. In the first four years of the Common Market's existence, according to Robert Marjolin of the Common Market Commission, the EEC increased its imports from the United States by 58 per cent. Each year the Six bought far more from the United States than they were able to sell in return. In 1962 the EEC trade deficit with the United States had been two billion dollars. This deficit had continued to rise in 1963. (OECD and American economists, calculating from a different basis, put the EEC deficit somewhat lower. But all agreed that the Six were sharply in the red in their trade with the United States.)

The average level of the Community's common external tariff, Marjolin continued, was "slightly below that of the American tariff." On the basis of its record, he contended, the Common Market's future trade policy should not be distrusted. "The Common Market," he said, "has given enough proof of its liberalism to be believed when it declares that it intends to take full account of the interests of friendly non-member countries in the final elaboration and implementation of its common agricultural policy." Beyond this the Six did not feel they could go.

These emerging problems were simply a result of the

Common Market's having grown up—a development which, on the whole, the United States greeted with joy. What made the problem difficult was that some people on both sides were being hurt. Between 1958 and 1962, for example, American poultry farmers increased their sales of frozen chickens to the Six from $2,800,000 to $52,000,000 a year. This was a bonanza for American farmers, plus their feed grain and other suppliers. It also helped to develop a taste for frozen chicken among European consumers. Consumption in West Germany almost trebled between 1958 and 1962.

Then the Six decided to develop a thriving poultry business of their own. To protect new producers the Common Market clamped on a higher levy—enough to drive American chickens out of much of their market. The United States retaliated by raising tariffs on certain EEC exports, equal in value to the amount of business lost by American poultry farmers. The incident, relatively small in itself, raised hackles because it was interpreted as an example of what might happen on a larger scale, when the common agricultural policy came into play. Common Market authorities denied such a correlation and sought to treat the "chicken war" on its own merits. They pointed out that no "traditional" American market was being lost, since the sales had developed almost from scratch since 1958.

In 1962 the United States raised tariffs on the import of woven carpets and flat glass, in response to the pleas of American manufacturers that they were being unfairly hurt by foreign competition. This decision was almost lost in the general flow of news and it is doubtful if many Americans ever noted the move. But to Belgian manufacturers of woven carpets it meant a great deal.

It turned out that many Belgian carpet factories were small family-type enterprises, almost wholly geared to sales in the

Petroleum is carried by barge on a Belgian canal

United States. They used American-made looms and other machinery, measured in feet and yards to accommodate American buyers, and sold about 80 per cent of their output in the United States. When the United States raised its tariff on woven carpets, 600 to 700 skilled Belgian carpet weavers lost their jobs.

United States officials regretted the hardship caused, but pointed out that this was somewhat a case of the shoe being on the other foot. In 1959 Belgium had drastically cut down its imports of United States coal, on the grounds that Belgium had a surplus of its own coal and was laying off Belgian miners. This situation still prevails, with Belgium buying about half as much American coal as it did before the cut-back. The United States Government complained but did not seek restitution, despite the fact that Belgian importers were breaking long-term contracts signed with coal producers in West Virginia—one of the poorest areas of the United States.

These human problems seemed bound to arise as the Common Market developed into a robust trading giant. The United States foresaw them and counted them less important than the over-all gain of a strong viable Western Europe. Many of the problems remain to be solved, particularly those of American farm sales to the Six. Some questions were threshed out in the "Kennedy Round" of GATT tariff negotiations which opened in Geneva in May 1964. Others, as they arise in the future, may be decided on a bilateral basis between the United States and the Six.

Even as it seeks to preserve the American position in European markets, the United States assures the Common Market of its continuing strong support. United States national interests are best served by a healthy Western Europe, despite short-term trade abrasions. This is the foundation from which the United States continues to work. All it asks is agreement that American producers will be able to compete among the Six for their traditional markets and, beyond that, to compete for a share of expanding markets, as Community trade grows.

To a remarkable degree private American firms have been coming to their own terms with the Common Market ever since the birth of that organization in 1958. Alert American businessmen foresaw the trade boom which the Common Market would bring about. They saw also the challenge posed to outsiders by elimination of internal trade barriers among the Six. The answer, to hundreds of American companies, was to become "insiders" themselves.

This they did. From January 1958 through April 1964, according to the Chase Manhattan Bank, 1,802 new business ventures were undertaken by American companies inside the Common Market. The most ambitious of these involved the building of manufacturing plants in Europe. A fruit-canning company in the United States, for example, would have to buck the common external tariff to sell its fruits among the Six. If that company built a processing plant in France or Italy, it would be inside the Common Market, benefiting from the progressive reduction of internal tariffs. From the standpoint of the host country the new factory meant jobs, a buyer of local fruits, and a source of tax income.

Other American companies bought up shares of European firms—sometimes a controlling share. A Frenchman buying a Simca automobile, a German buying an Opel or a Taunus, were acquiring cars with European names. In fact, the companies that built them were largely owned by American capital.

Other American firms granted licenses to European companies to manufacture American products according to U.S. specifications. An American housewife in Holland might be delighted to find American brand names on the shelves of Dutch grocers and druggists. Picking up the familiar box or can, she would read: Made in the Netherlands, or France, or West Germany, as the case might be.

Among the Six, France led the way in attracting American investment ventures, with 480 entries between 1958 and April 1964. Tiny Belgium and Luxembourg came next, with 371 between them. Eskimo Pie was one American company that chose Luxembourg as the site of its Common Market venture. Italy attracted 362 American firms, West Germany 351, and the Netherlands 238, for a grand Common Market total of 1,802.

This was the lion's share of all American investment ventures in Western Europe during the period under study. The seven nations of EFTA attracted 627 American investments during the same period, with Britain acquiring 284, followed by Switzerland with 270. The other five EFTA partners (Denmark, Norway, Sweden, Austria, and Portugal) shared out 75 American investment ventures among them. (On a per capita basis of population EFTA did better than the figures might indicate. The seven EFTA partners among them had 90,000,000 persons, against 170,000,000 for the six nations of the Common Market.) American investment in Britain probably would have been higher, had the latter become a member of the EEC. Some United States firms had hoped to use Britain as a base for penetrating the Common Market, while others, already established within the Community, had looked to expansion of their activity in England.

During the early years of the Common Market, American companies rushed in to stake out a claim. This initial scramble to enter the European market appears to be over. For one thing, hundreds of the most obvious investment opportunities long ago were combed over and snapped up by large American companies. The saturation point of American firms within the Common Market is approaching. Also, inflation in all EEC countries except West Germany somewhat reduced European profit margins.

Companies already within the Common Market are concerned to consolidate the hold they secured in the early days of investment. This they are doing through various types of joint ventures with European companies. A French firm, for example, might be strong within France, but weak outside. To team up with a large American company with outlets elsewhere in the Common Market might help both to expand. Some European firms also are seeking to broaden their product line, by associating with American companies that sell a related or different range of goods.

On the whole, according to a Chase Manhattan study, American management likes to buy into European firms, with option to buy up majority control. This approach is opposed by many European businessmen and by some governments. The preference among Europeans is to pool American and European resources in wholly new third companies, whose operations are somewhat insulated from the parents.

The current period of American investment in Europe is considered mature, or sophisticated. The experimental toe-hold was made long ago. Confidence in the durability of the Common Market now is causing American management to look toward careful long-range expansion, in co-operation with European capital. There is even a beginning interest among European businessmen to invest their surplus capital and capacity in the United States. Truly such businessmen, aided by the American example, have learned the lesson of the Common Market—to aim at a huge market, beyond national frontiers.

The Iron Curtain Cracks

Over the years the Soviet Union, on the other side of the ideological fence, has watched the Common Market—first deriding the unity efforts of the Six, then growing pensive, as it were, and finally alarmed. The success of the Common Market posed a challenge to the Soviet bloc, whose economies were in serious trouble during the early and mid-1960's.

"Fiasco," was the official comment of the Soviet Government in 1958, when the European Economic Community was born. This merger, according to the Soviets, was nothing more than the economic foundation of NATO's struggle against the Socialist countries. ("Socialist" is the word used by Communist governments to describe themselves.) This "merger of monopolies" was aimed against the working classes. The result of the Common Market would be increased unemployment, a reduction in real income, and the reinforcement of United States control in Europe. This was the analysis of the Soviet Institute of World Economics.

It soon became clear that the analysis did not fit the facts. Unemployment among the Six, far from increasing, disappeared almost altogether. France depended on Spanish,

Italian masons working in Munich, West Germany

Portuguese, and Algerian workers to fill vacant jobs, particularly manual labor. Italian workers flooded into West Germany until Italy's own economic boom drew many of them back. In 1964 West Germany welcomed its one millionth foreign worker. Wages skyrocketed among the Six—too quickly, in fact, as employers outbid each other for scarce labor. The United States, far from dominating the Common Market, began to fear the loss of its traditional markets.

*Housing built by the Coal and Steel Community
for workers in Luxembourg*

Communists as well as non-Communists were benefiting from all this. Many workers in Italy and France belonged to the Communist Party. Yet their incomes soared, along with those of everyone else. The Communist Party of Italy felt forced to point out that the vitality and production increases of the Common Market could not be denied.

This posed Moscow with a major problem. According to Marxist dialectic, world capitalism was in a crisis, born of a struggle among monopolists, within which the working classes were being ground down. How to explain the contradictory experience of the EEC? In September 1962 Soviet

Premier Nikita S. Khrushchev took a preliminary step. He published an article in the "World Marxist Review," in which he acknowledged that the Common Market was here to stay.

Communists, he said, must continue to point out the "dangerous consequences" of the Common Market to workers. None the less, Khrushchev wrote, the "rulers of the Western world, notwithstanding all their antagonisms, have partly succeeded in forming inter-State alliances" and had achieved "international economic co-operation in a number of important spheres." This being the case, the Communist bloc must be prepared to establish businesslike contacts with it.

This was followed in September 1963 by a conference of Communist economic experts, devoted to a study of the Common Market. These experts acknowledged that the EEC constituted a new economic reality, which had changed the balance of power between Europe and the United States. Communists now must struggle, it was said, against the attempt of capitalistic forces to use this new economic power to strengthen the position of international monopolists and to prepare for war by increasing armaments. Above all, the Common Market must be recognized as an obstacle to the expansion of world trade.

This last was a key to Communist concern. Despite their ideological fulminations against the Common Market, almost every state of the Communist bloc, including the Soviet Union, was eager to trade with the Six. Western Europe could supply the advanced technology—the chemical and fertilizer factories, synthetic fabric plants, and heavy machine tools—which the Iron Curtain countries urgently needed to modernize their economies.

Bad crop years in the early 1960's had forced Communist governments to spend hundreds of millions of dollars of scarce foreign currency reserves to buy wheat from Canada, the United States, and elsewhere in the free world. Communist agriculture required vast investment in chemical fertilizer plants, if its crop yields were to be stabilized. The Six, as well as Britain, could supply these factories. It was the manner of payment that was the rub.

Eighteen Western nations, including the United States and all members of the EEC, had banded together in the so-called Bern Union, one of whose objects became to deny long-term credits to the Communist bloc. The reason for this was to force Soviet bloc governments to make at least a limited choice between guns and butter. It worked like this. Suppose the Soviet Union wished to buy fifty million dollars' worth of industrial equipment from the West. It might approach a large Western company, or group of companies, and offer to pay for the equipment over a period of fifteen years, at 4 per cent interest. This would mean that the Soviets would not have to pay out the fifty million dollars all at once, but could dribble it out over a long period of time, paying 4 per cent extra for this privilege. It also might mean that the Soviets could spend part of that money on guns, or nuclear bombs, in the meantime.

Such long-term credit deals are common among friendly free world countries. India, for example, might offer to buy fifty million dollars' worth of equipment from an American company on fifteen-year credit terms. The American firm would agree, if it could be insured against loss. The United States Government, to help this American company land the business against foreign competitors, would guarantee the company against loss over the fifteen-year period. The governments of most major industrial countries have such credit insurance programs, to aid their businessmen.

One object of the Bern Union agreement was to prevent Communist governments from obtaining long-term credit guarantees of this type. Five years was set as the maximum credit which the West would offer. This would force the Communists to spend cash for many of the things they wanted to buy in the West. Either they would have to dip into their currency reserves, or they would have to sell goods of their own to earn the money.

As a result, most Communist bloc trade with the West was negotiated through bilateral trade deals. That is, the Soviet Government might agree to buy one hundred million dollars' worth of goods from West Germany each year, if the Germans bought an equivalent amount of Soviet products, perhaps coal, cotton, and wool. Often such deals included the "most favored nation" clause. This meant that the two signatories promised to grant each other the most favorable tariff terms they were giving to any other trading partner.

This was before the establishment of the Common Market. After 1958 no one of the Six could grant as favorable terms to any outside power as it was giving to its partners within the EEC. In 1963 the Soviet Government approached several members of the Six separately, seeking special tariff concessions on certain Russian exports, including caviar. Each of the Six thus approached referred the request to Common Market headquarters in Brussels, explaining to Moscow that an EEC government was not a free agent in this respect.

The Council of Ministers, having deliberated on the Soviet request, replied in effect: "We might be able to give you what you ask. The Common Market Commission is at your disposal for negotiations." Since that time, according to EEC authorities, there has been only silence from Moscow. To have agreed to negotiate with the Commission would have meant official recognition of the European Economic Community by the Soviet Union. This Moscow has been unwilling to give.

But trade pressures on the Soviet bloc continue to grow.

Russia's trade with the Six amounts to only about 10 per cent of the Soviet Union's total foreign commerce. The same is roughly true for other members of the Communist bloc. But this 10 per cent is of crucial importance to the Communists. It involves the modern industrial equipment which only the West can provide.

To ease the Communist dilemma, Khrushchev sought, before his removal from power, a tightening of economic co-operation, somewhat along the lines of the Common Market, among the member countries of the economic organization of the Sino-Soviet bloc. This organization, known as the Council for Mutual Economic Assistance (CMEA, or Comecon), includes the Soviet Union, Bulgaria, Czechoslovakia, East Germany, Hungary, Poland, Romania, and Outer Mongolia. Communist China, North Korea, and North Vietnam have "observer" status in Comecon.

But Comecon is powerless to accomplish for the Iron Curtain countries what the Common Market is doing for the Six. The economies of the Communist countries simply are not complementary. They cannot supply and support each other's needs. All of them, in varying degree, must import their technology from the West. Furthermore, the struggle between the Soviet Union and Communist China to control the world Communist movement undercuts the possibility of bloc co-operation.

Finally, there is a growing spirit of independence among Eastern European governments as they strive to break out of economic backwardness. Romania refused outright to submit its economic development to Soviet control. Seeking "only the best," the Romanian Government in June 1964 concluded a trade agreement with the United States, under which the Romanians plan to buy a wide range of American industrial equipment. Other members of Comecon, notably

Hungary and Poland, are forging closer trade ties with Western countries.

Meanwhile, as economic pressures deepen, Moscow continues to pump out the policy line that the Common Market is reactionary and imperialist, directed against Communist countries, against the underdeveloped nations of the world, and against the interests of workers and farmers. Manifestly, this is untrue. Eighteen governments of Negro Africa have found it beneficial to associate with the EEC. Working classes among the Six are prospering as never before.

The Soviet Government is shrewdly trying to break the Bern Union ban on the granting of long-term Western credits to the Communist bloc. With Britain, France, and to some extent Italy, the Soviets have succeeded. If this Western breach widens, Moscow's need to negotiate directly with the EEC might be postponed. The advantage to the Soviets of extended credit terms might outweigh the disadvantage of having to hurdle the common external tariff of the Common Market.

Eventually, however, the growing influence of the Community would seem bound to propel the Soviets toward a decision they have avoided—sending a diplomatic mission to the EEC Commission in Brussels, as fifty-eight other nations have done. This would be a defeat for Soviet propaganda and Marxist doctrine. But if Moscow hesitates too long, its hand may be forced by some of its restless satellites.

Where Will the Future Lead?

If the Common Market ever develops an agency whose function is to impress the outsider, I suggest that it encourage visitors to disembark at the Belgian port of Ostend and drive eastward through Bruges, Ghent, Antwerp, and down to Brussels. After that ride the visitor will be prepared to believe almost any statistics on Western Europe's prosperity that are thrust upon him.

The traveler rolls through miles of suburban streets lined with handsome brick houses, each of which would have cost $40,000 or more in the United States. The houses are amazingly individual in design, except that each contains one central similarity—a gigantic picture window, behind whose green-tinted glass a huge Delft or Chinese vase is exactly centered. Each of these Belgian homes is spaciously set within its own manicured lawn and garden. Two-car garages housing French, German, or American automobiles are not uncommon. Belgium, the visitor concludes, is a country whose burghers know how to live. To an American, this looks like prosperity as he knows it in the United States.

Then the traveler penetrates further among the Six and

New apartment in Brussels reflects growing prosperity

his doubts begin to grow. He finds graceful old cities, full of narrow streets, fronted by tall, often shabby-looking apartment houses. As architecture, these apartment houses may be picturesque. As places to live in, they are something else. Their ill-lighted stairways lead up to small flats whose kitchens are cramped and whose bathrooms often are nonexistent. The back of each flat opens out on an inner court of unrelieved gray gloom.

Cities in every country of the Six are marked by streets and houses such as these, varying somewhat, of course, according to the neighborhood and nationality. In such apartments live millions of the people of the Six. The visitor

*Europe on your plate—a Brussels department store
sells foods of the Six*

goes to Paris, queen city of the West, and marvels at its
broad boulevards and open sweeps of view, its churches,
bridges, and squares of splendor. Then he learns that, even
today, nearly half of all Parisians have neither running hot
water nor private bathroom facilities in their homes!

Where, he might ask, is this prosperity, this bursting
economic strength, of which he has heard so much? It is
there, but the buildings themselves often do not show it.
These cities of Europe were built in an earlier slower age
when carriages, not cars, competed on the roads. Few people
foresaw that one day the narrow crooked streets of Europe,
developed often from cart tracks, would be jammed bumper

to bumper by gasoline-powered vehicles, while European merchants continued to set up their outdoor stalls on curbings and shoppers milled about the streets, as their forebears had done for centuries past.

To reconstruct such cities would be a mammoth undertaking. Even to install new plumbing or a more modern furnace in a crumbling shell of a building is enough to give an owner pause. Will it be worth it? Or should he continue to patch along, until one day he can afford to move outside the city or until the government decides to broaden his street? These are reasons why housing is one of the last things to change in Europe's economic boom.

Once during World War II, I was stationed for a week in a small French town outside Nancy, near the German border. The town was still shuttered up from the hardships of war and occupation. For our regiment it was a "rest" time. There was little to do but wander the silent streets and wait for our next move. Every detail of the flat in which I was billeted impressed itself upon my thought.

Nineteen years later my family and I had occasion to drive through that same French town, now cheerful and bustling. Memories began to stir and we searched out the square where I had lived. There stood the tall apartment house, with the same heavy oak door that I remembered. I mounted the sagging wooden stairs (they had sagged nineteen years before) to the third floor flat. The new owners heard my story and graciously welcomed me in.

In one room I saw the huge old armoire, or movable closet, in which I had hung my uniforms. That had been passed along from one owner to the next. In the living room, or salon, as the French call it, the same windows with their massive bronze knobs looked down upon the square. Within the house itself little seemed to have changed, except that the owners were ripping off the faded wallpaper to repaint the walls themselves.

But outside in the square stood a brisk little European car, bright in the sunshine. That belonged to the owner. So did a gleaming new refrigerator in the kitchen, the joy of his wife. Here was the key to this family's prosperity. They were concentrating, not on the apartment itself, but on the consumer goods with which they lived in that house—refrigerator, vacuum cleaner, television set, and, outside in the square, a little car with which to picnic in the country on weekends.

So it is all over Western Europe. Television aerials sprout from old gabled roofs, amid the chimney pots. Refrigerators stand in hallways, because there is no room for them in the kitchens. These are the ways, scarcely visible to the casual tourist, in which prosperity is measured among the peoples of the Six.

In 1961 I looked at an apartment for rent near the Bois de Boulogne in Paris, a fashionable district of distinguished old flats. In the salon hung a chandelier of crystal, above a fine Persian rug. The furniture in the dining room was massive and obviously expensive. But in the tiny kitchen I looked in vain for the refrigerator, thinking of the large model with built-in freezer we were bringing over from the States. "Where do you keep your refrigerator?" I asked the lady of the house, a modish Parisienne with bouffant hairdo.

"Oh, we have none!" she replied. This well-to-do lady, like thousands of her poorer sisters throughout Paris, went out once or twice each day to small neighborhood shops to buy enough milk, cheese, butter, meat, and vegetables for that day's meals. What else could she do, since she had no place to keep her food cold? Her apartment, an "elegant" address in Paris, had not been built to accommodate a refrigerator.

New construction in Rotterdam

Outside many cities of Europe new blocks of flats are going up, built around their own stores, like suburban shopping centers in the United States. In these new apartments the kitchens are larger, with space provided for refrigerator and gas or electric stove. Available in almost every shopping center is a busy supermarket, where European housewives, like their counterparts in the United States, can trundle carts among the shelves and stock up for several days. This is the coming "new look" in Europe. But it will take a long time to catch up with the housing needs of growing populations.

How much of this consumer prosperity would have come about by itself and how much is due to the Common Market?

Economists of the Six ask themselves this and are puzzled. There is no exact way of knowing. But all agree that the existence of the Common Market has played a major role. In France, for example, some of the most ambitious super-markets are partly Belgian-owned. Would those Belgian owners have decided to build in France, if the Community had not existed? Perhaps, but through much more red tape and with higher prices—and a narrower range of goods—on their shelves.

I asked an Italian diplomat what effect the Common Market had had upon the economy of his country. "Between 1958 and 1963," he replied, "trade between Italy and France multiplied five times. It might have grown, but not so much, without the Common Market." That was one way of putting it. Another way is the fact that in 1963 more Italian refrigerators were being sold in France than those made in any other country—including France. The Italian machines were hand-some, efficient, and they were entering France free of quota and at low duties, thanks to the Common Market. They were coming in just as the French people, riding the boom of French prosperity, were becoming refrigerator-conscious.

So stiff was the competition for French refrigerator makers that the French Government asked the Common Market Commission for permission to charge a temporary duty on the Italian machines, until the French industry had had time to adjust. This was a tribute to Italian refrigerators. But it was also a tribute to the practical results of eliminating trade barriers among the Six. Permission was granted—for a limited period of time. The temporary tax has ended and French refrigerator makers now are on their own.

I went into a Paris department store to buy a raincoat. The model the salesgirl urged upon me as the best value for my money had been made in Italy. The little creamery near our home outside Paris carried two brands of cookies we particularly liked. One was made in Belgium, the other in Holland. A young Frenchwoman summed it up, during the marathon struggle over agriculture among the Six, when the future existence of the Community seemed in doubt. "I just can't imagine," she said, "going into a store and not having a choice from other countries!"

This is why the Common Market, in the view of almost all authorities, is here to stay. It has entered into the warp and woof of everyday life in Western Europe. Consumers of the Six are geared to the Common Market. Equally important, so are farmers and manufacturers. They have retooled their planning, their expectations, and in many cases the assembly lines of their factories, to a greatly expanded market. They simply could not shrink back within national frontiers without painful readjustments. No government is likely to ask them to do so.

In 1963, according to the Common Market Commission, trade of all kinds within the Community expanded by 17 per cent over 1962. Intra-Community trade in private consumer goods—clothing, cars, washing machines, radios, and the like—was 46 per cent higher than it had been in 1960. In the same period the Six had expanded their imports of consumer goods from non-member countries by only 27 per cent. Obviously, consumers of the Six were looking to each other's goods at an increasing rate, as internal tariffs dropped toward zero.

"We are sure," Professor Hallstein wrote in a statement to the author, "that the EEC has passed the point of no return. The degree to which the Community has now grown together makes all retreat impossible, for the great economic area which is emerging has already become the basis of innumerable individual decisions and thus entered into the

Merchants of the Six adopt European signs

very structure of our European economy ... The six member countries have committed themselves to pooling their economic and political destinies. All of them have a big stake in the Community and will benefit from its steady development. For them there is no practical political alternative to European integration."

Hallstein did not mean that problems would not arise in the future. "It is clear," he wrote, "that the far-reaching process of integration will not be carried through without crises and difficulties. Major interests are at stake in the member countries and, as we progress toward economic union, agreement will often require courageous political decisions."

One difficulty with which the Six currently are grappling is inflation. As President de Gaulle told the French people, in urging upon them his government's price stabilization plan: "The European Common Market ... would not long incorporate a French economy" weakened by inflation. As the dikes of internal protection go down, inflation in one Community partner becomes a threat to the others. For this reason inflation, while a danger, has had the effect of forcing the Six into co-operative financial and monetary action faster than they had expected.

Also disturbing to Common Market experts is the fact that the Six, taken as a whole, suffer from a balance of trade deficit with the outside world. That is, the six EEC partners buy more goods from non-member countries than they sell in return. In 1963 this trade deficit amounted to three billion dollars and the next year the figure crept higher. This should not be confused with the over-all balance of payments. When all other factors were counted in, including receipts from tourism and investment of foreign capital, the Six still possessed a total payments surplus. Thus France, for example, was able to add to its foreign exchange reserves, even though French trade was running in the red.

In part the balance of trade problem was linked to inflation. Some EEC governments had felt forced to lower duties on imports, in an effort to impel domestic manufacturers to keep their prices low, or at least competitive. Also, prosperity among the Six had created a strong buyers' demand that had boosted imports of consumer goods. In the long run, according to Commission experts, a continuing trade deficit was not healthy. Although currently cushioned by their over-all balance of payments surplus, the Six must work toward bringing their sales of goods into balance with their imports.

Problems like inflation and a deficit balance of trade are economic, such as might arise in any large trading community. To forewarn members and help steer them through such economic shoals, the Common Market Commission promised to "maintain a close watch on the development of the situation in each of the member countries," so that the Commission might make recommendations "at any moment." Each member government, preoccupied primarily with its own problems, could count on a supranational watchdog keeping an eye on the co-ordinated development of the Community as a whole.

Apart from these questions is the roadblock to political unity among the Six, stemming primarily from the difference of view between President de Gaulle and his partners. Paul Henri Spaak of Belgium declared bluntly in 1964 that at present there was "little chance of further progress toward political unity in Europe. The difference in approach is so great and so profound that it is difficult to conceive of anyone proposing a compromise, let alone accepting one. This is just not the time."

None the less, Spaak felt not unduly pessimistic. "We

The busy port at Rotterdam

have the Common Market and its achievements to hold on to," he affirmed. "It provides a solid rock to which we must hold fast and on which . . . we must build our hopes for the future. If, in the economic sphere, we continue to make progress at the same rate as in the last few years . . . there will be good reason to hope that the tying together of our economic interests will one day make clear to everyone the absolute necessity for a political authority. I do not like a policy of waiting, except when it is imposed on me, but I believe that this time history is with us and that it is leading us unavoidably to unity."

This echoed Jean Monnet's conviction that, confronted by a political roadblock, the Community must expand its economic unity, step by step. Each step thus gained would unfold the way to the next. The essential thing was to have concrete institutions in place, administering each step and insulated from control by any single government.

During the first seven years of the operation of the Common Market and of Euratom, and throughout the first twelve years of the Coal and Steel Community, this function had been performed by the three executive commissions.

The Council of Ministers now authorized a dramatic forward step. The three separate commissions were to be merged into one, to administer all three communities. This

Sicco Mansholt (left) chats with Edgard Pisani,
French Minister of Agriculture

meant that the High Authority of the ECSC and the commissions of the Common Market and Euratom would disappear in their present form, to be replaced by a single new
body. This would be followed by the merger of the three
communities them selves at the beginning of 1967. No longer
would there be one community handling coal and steel,
another atomic energy, and a third other fields of economic
integration. All would be combined within a single community, administered by a single executive group.

To Monnet, this was an important move. Automatically
the authority of such a single executive would be increased,
even though it received no specific new powers. It would loom
over the economy of Europe in a more concentrated fashion
than the three separate commissions could do. Paralleling
this step would be the final elimination of internal customs
duties among the Six.

These steps had been officially approved. Beyond them,
Monnet and his Action Committee for a United States of
Europe suggested other moves. Monnet urged that the chairman of the combined executives should be elected by the
European Parliament. This would be done through consultation between the six governments and representatives of the
parliament. From the list of candidates thus put forward, the
assembly would elect the chairman of the executive. He then
would have an increased insularity from any single government and a more direct mandate from the people.

Monnet also believed that one-half the deputies of the
European Parliament should be elected directly by the people.
The parliament would be doubled from its present size of
142 members. This would leave the same number of deputies
as at present to be appointed by their respective national parliaments. The other 142 would be elected directly by the
people from European lists. The Socialist parties of the Six

would put up a "European slate" of Socialists. The Christian Democrats and other parties would do the same. Thus voters in West Germany, or Holland, might be voting for deputies from Italy or France.

By such institutional steps, Monnet was convinced, the EEC would approach full unity, one step at a time. De Gaulle, he pointed out, originally had been against the Common Market. Now the French President was for it. De Gaulle had been opposed to giving power to the "technocrats" of the executives. Now the French Government supported the fusion of the three. Why? Because experience had made a success, for France itself, of the Common Market.

One morning in March 1962 huge signs appeared outside a Paris department store. Painted like packing cases, the signs read: "France and the Common Market." Salesmen at sidewalk stalls held up ballpoint pens and hawked their wares like carnival barkers. "Pens of the Common Market! Made in France, Germany, Italy! Buy them here, six for ten francs (two dollars)!"

Inside the store, as the shopper glided up the escalator, a soft voice intoned: "On the fifth floor, France and the Common Market!" Displayed on the walls were the sides of packing cases, plastered with names: Le Havre, Antwerp, Milan, Cologne, the ports and cities of the Six. Pretty French girls in Dutch national costume sold cheeses from Holland. A display of bright straw hats and bags from Italy bloomed like flowers, while a fifth-floor newsstand sold the latest newspapers from all over Western Europe. Flags of six nations blossomed on the walls.

Featured were sixty-two "Champions of Europe," products singled out because the Common Market had drastically reduced their prices since 1958, making them bargains for

Signs reading "France and the Common Market" advertise wares from the Six on sale at a department store in Paris.

the European consumer. A sign said: "Electric clock, value in 1958, 69 francs ($14.00), price today 42.50 ($8.50)." Another read: "Automatic pencil, four colors, 1958 value 19.50 francs ($4.00), price today 12.50 ($2.50)." A woman's raincoat from Italy, $22.00 in 1958, $8.00 today. A French stainless steel cooking set, $24.00 in 1958, $14.00 today.

Nationality of the goods was not stressed, for the store was interested in selling the products, not the country that made them. But if one searched, he found that among the sixty-two "Champions of Europe" were thirty-six French products, sixteen Italian, seven German, two Belgian, and one Dutch.

On the metro going home, it was easy to pick out who had been shopping at the "Common Market." Those with multicolored bags marked "France and the Common Market" were good advertisements for the store—and for the exciting, increasingly down-to-earth economic integration of Europe.

Each year on February 21 elderly French war veterans still gather around the flag to rekindle memories of Verdun. They have come to pay tribute to their fallen comrades. But their meetings, lessening in number year by year, also hark back to the old Europe, whose enmities resulted in the Battle of Verdun.

The store in Paris was celebrating a new Europe. Since that sale in 1962 tariffs have tumbled a further 40 per cent within the Common Market. Stores all over the Six stock products from each other's lands. Workers of the Community travel freely across frontiers. Children are learning history from a European standpoint.

One French town near Lyons has renamed itself—Grezieu-la-Varenne, Commune de l'Europe, or district of Europe. The mayor put up a new sign with these words at the entrance to town, because young people of Grezieu, in answering a questionnaire, had said they thought of themselves as "Europeans." In a leaflet distributed to citizens of the town, Mayor Joel Chotard explained: "I have had this sign put up simply to remind everyone that progress, freedom, and peace are only possible in a united and integrated Europe of which France is a part . . ."

One man of the town, a veteran of World War I, added his thoughts. "In the trenches, where I saw so much suffering,

I was already asking myself the question: 'Why can't Europe be united like America?' I'm glad to see that my old dream is going to come true at last."

The dream will take years to complete. But six European countries have come a long way since that day in 1950 when Robert Schuman stood up in the Quai d'Orsay in Paris to read an end to violence along the Rhine.

Index

(Asterisks indicate illustrations)

ABC weapons, 34, 56
Acheson, Dean, 161
Action Committee for a United States of Europe, 59–60, 61, 111, 193
Adenauer, Konrad, 12, 12*, 29, 44, 63*
Africa, 87, 89. *See also* Association Convention.
    colonial, 82–83, 84*n*.
    independent states, 84
Algeria, 123–124
Alsace, 21–22, 23, 25, 29, 40, 43. *See also* Lorraine.
Armand, Louis, 111*n*.
Association Convention, 84, 84*n*, 85*, 86
Austria, 22, 23, 148, 154–155, 158

balance of payments, 35, 36, 67–68, 162, 165, 189–190
balance of trade, 189–190
Belgium, 15, 16, 32, 37, 44, 55, 62, 133, 166, 167*, 180
Benelux countries, 37, 48, 65

Berlin blockade (1948), 32
Bern Union, 176, 179
Beyen, Johan Willem, 58
Bismarck, Otto von, 23
Britain. *See* Great Britain.
Brussels, 73, 75, 112
Brussels Treaty (1948), 32

Charlemagne, 17, 18, 18*, 19
Charles Martel (Charles the Hammer), 17, 18
Charles the Bald, 17, 20
Charles the Fat, 21
Churchill, Winston, 27, 32, 39–40
Coal, 16, 40, 42, 48, 49, 50, 167–168. *See also* European Coal and Steel Community.
Common Market (European Economic Community), 15, 52, 61–89, 134–136, 140, 143–144, 153–155, 163, 192. *See also* Treaty of Rome.
    Africa, 82–83, 84, 86, 87, 89
    agriculture, 99–102, 103, 104, 105, 105*, 106, 107, 108, 133

consumers, 61, 62n., 66, 187
foreign investment, 70, 168–171
Great Britain, 137–155
headquarters, 73, 74*
merchants, 16, 182*, 186, 188*
Soviet Union, 172–175, 177–179
stages, 64, 79, 80–81
trade 62n., 69–70, 165
United States, 157–159, 163–164, 168
Common Market Commission, 72–73, 77–79, 101, 138
members, 72–73
Commonwealth, British, 138, 139, 144, 146, 148, 149*, 150, 152, 153
Congress of Europe, 29
Consultative Committee, 46
Council for Mutual Economic Assistance (CMEA), 178
Council of Europe, 29–31, 37, 48
headquarters, 29
members, 30n.
Council of Ministers, 46, 47, 48, 64, 71, 78, 79, 81, 100, 104, 192
Court of Justice, 46, 48, 71, 78, 129
headquarters, 46
Cuba, 131
customs union, 62, 64–65, 69, 86, 192

de Gasperi, Alcide, 29, 44
de Gaulle, Charles, 12, 12*, 29, 40, 55, 189
Algerian policy, 123–124
and Common Market, 131, 133, 134–136
farm policy, 102, 103, 107, 108
and Great Britain, 137, 138, 139, 140, 143, 146

nationalism, 38, 42, 122–136
and NATO, 120, 125–131, 132
President, 124*, 125
World War II leader, 123
de Murville, Maurice Couve, 143
Denmark, 137, 140
DRAGON project, 119
Dunkirk Treaty (1947), 32

Economic Cooperation Administration, 36. See also Marshall Plan.
Economic and Social Committee, 78
ECSC. See European Coal and Steel Community.
EEC. See European Economic Community, Common Market, and Treaty of Rome.
EFTA. See European Free Trade Association.
Eisenhower, Dwight D., 33, 125, 129
Erhard, Ludwig, 107, 133
Etzel, Franz, 111n.
Euratom (European Atomic Energy Community), 52, 61, 109, 110*, 111–121, 140, 192
and France, 120–121
headquarters, 110*
nuclear power stations, 112, 113*
nuclear research, 113–114, 114*, 115, 115*, 116, 119
Euratom Supply Agency, 112
"Eurocrats," 75
Europe
early history, 17, 19, 21, 26, 29
post World War II, 33, 35, 41, 42, 44, 143
European Agricultural Guidance

and Guarantee Fund, 102, 103, 105

European Army, 54–55

European Coal and Steel Community (ECSC), 43, 44, 46–53, 54, 61, 192. *See also* Schuman Plan.
    members, 44

European Commission on Human Rights, 30–31

European Convention on Human Rights, 30, 30*n.*, 31

European Court, 30–31, 48

European Defense Community (EDC), 54, 56, 58

European Development Fund for Overseas, 84

European Economic Community (EEC), 29, 61, 63, 64, 74, 140. *See also* Common Market.

European Free Trade Area, 145–146

European Free Trade Association (EFTA), 147, 148, 152, 153–154, 170

European Investment Bank, 82

European Labor Exchange, 80

European Parliament, 46, 47, 71, 78, 141–142, 142*, 193

European Political Community (EPC), 54, 55

"European Schools," 76, 76*, 77, 77*

European Social Fund, 81

European unity
    Action Committee, 59, 111, 193
    early trends, 26, 27, 28–29

famers, 90–108
    British, 150–151, 152

French, 90–91, 95–98, 98*, 99

West German, 96, 99–100, 104, 106, 107, 108, 140

United States, 163, 165, 187

farming, 94, 97*, 98*, 99

farms, 91*, 92, 94, 95, 96, 98

France
    agriculture, 104–106, 107, 108
    colonies, 82–85
    early history, 11, 15, 16, 21, 22, 23, 25
    industry, 134*, 135*
    post World War II, 32, 42, 44, 62, 67

General Agreement on Tariffs and Trade (GATT), 36, 65, 164, 168

German War of Liberation (1813), 23

Germany, 16, 19, 21, 22, 23, 25, 33, 42. *See also* West Germany.

Giordani, Francesco, 111*n.*

grain, 96, 103, 105–106, 107–108, 164

Great Britain, 32, 55, 56, 61, 103, 133, 144
    and Common Market, 137–140, 141*, 142–155
    and ECSC, 145
    and EFTA, 147–48

Greece, 87–88, 147

Green Report, 93, 96

Hallstein, Walter, 72, 73*, 79, 140, 143, 152, 187, 188, 189

Heath, Edward, 143

High Authority of Common Market, 43, 44, 46–47, 47*, 48, 49–52, 71, 72
    headquarters, 46*

Hitler, Adolf, 17, 25

Holland, 15, 29, 44, 86. *See also* Netherlands, The.
Holy Roman Empire, 21, 22
House of Europe, The, 4*, 29, 31, 46
House of Hohenzollern, 22
housing, 51, 66, 67, 174*, 180–181, 181*, 182–185, 185*
Hungary, 179

IBRD. *See* International Bank for Reconstruction and Development.
IMF. *See* International Monetary Fund.
Indo-China, 53
inflation, 66–67, 69, 189, 190
"Inner Six," 147
International Bank for Reconstruction and Development (IBRD), 36
International Committee of the Movements for European Unity, 29
International Monetary Fund (IMF), 36
Iran, 88–89
Ireland, Republic of, 137–138, 140
iron, 16, 40, 48, 49
Israel, 88–89
Italy, 15, 42, 44, 62

Kennedy, John F., 71, 127, 131, 139, 159, 160, 160*, 161, 162
Korean War (1950), 53
Khrushchev, Nikita S., 175, 178

Latin America, 86, 87
Les Halles, 94, 95*, 95
Lorraine, 13, 15, 20, 22, 23, 25, 40, 43. *See also* Alsace.

Lothair, 17, 20, 20*
Lotharingia, 20, 21
Louis XIV, King, of France, 22
Louis the German, 17, 20, 21
Luxembourg, 15, 32, 37, 44, 55, 62

Macmillan, Harold, 139, 148
Malvestiti, Pietro, 140
Mansholt, Sicco L., 105, 106, 107*, 192*
Marjolin, Robert, 68, 68*, 165
Marshall, George C., 35
Marshall Plan, 35–36, 126, 157. *See also* Economic Cooperation Administration.
Mayer, René, 58
Mendes-France, Pierre, 55
Messina conference, 58, 60
miners, coal, 49, 50*, 52*
    retraining, 51
Monnet, Jean, 28
    Action Committee, 59–60, 61, 192, 193
    career, 38–39, 40, 41, 41*, 42
    Common Market, 58–59, 61
    ECSC, 43–46, 57
    Euratom, 61, 111
    and Great Britain, 139, 145

Napoleon, 17, 22–23
NATO. *See* North Atlantic Treaty Organization.
Netherlands, The, 32, 37, 44, 55, 62, 133
North Atlantic Treaty (1949), 32, 35
North Atlantic Treaty Organization (NATO), 33, 34, 36, 53, 56, 120, 125, 126, 127–130, 139
    members, 33*n*.
nuclear fission, 119

nuclear fusion, 119

OECD. *See* Organization for Economic Cooperation and Development.
OEEC. *See* Organization for European Economic Cooperation.
Ollenhauer, Erich, 59
Organization for Economic Cooperation and Development (OECD), 36, 88, 163
   members, 36*n*.
Organization for European Economic Cooperation (OEEC), 35–36
"Outer Seven," 147

Partition of Verdun (843), 21, 23
Pepin the Short, 17–19
"pieds noirs," 124
Pisani, Edgard, 108, 193
Poland, 179
Pompidou, Georges, 12*, 97, 137
Prussia, 22, 23

quota restrictions, 63, 64

Rhine River, 15, 20, 22, 25, 26, 197
Romania, 178
Rotterdam, 191*
Ruhr, 40, 42, 43
Russia. *See* Soviet Union.

Saar, 45
Sassen, E.M.J.A., 141
Schuman, Robert, 40, 41*, 44, 45, 197
Schuman Plan, 40, 44, 54. *See also* European Coal and Steel Community.
Schwarz, Werner, 106

Scientific and Technical Committee, 112
Sforza, Carlo, 44
Six, the
   and Africa, 86
   agriculture, 100–101, 102, 103, 108
   budget, 67–69, 79
   Common Market, 61, 62, 63, 66, 67, 69–70
   ECSC, 46, 47, 50, 58
   Euratom, 61, 111, 112-113
   and Great Britain, 138
   prosperity, 184, 185–186
South Vietnam, 162
Southwest Experimental Fast Oxide Reactor, 118
Soviet Institute of World Economics, 172
Soviet Union, 36, 41, 53, 126, 131, 156
   agriculture, 176
   and Bern Union, 176, 179
   and Common Market, 172-175, 177–179
   European satellites, 32, 36
   Sino-Soviet bloc, 178, 179
Spaak, Paul Henri, 28, 28*, 44, 58–59, 60, 61, 63*, 109, 190–191
Spain, 88
steel, 42, 48, 49, 154*. *See also* European Coal and Steel Community.
Strasbourg, 20, 22, 24, 24*, 25, 29, 46
Sweden, 148, 158
Switzerland, 30*n*., 148, 158

tariffs
   British, 148–149, 153
   colonies, 83, 86

common external, 65, 89, 119, 147, 153, 165
the Six, 43, 62, 63, 64, 187
United States, 65, 89, 163, 165, 166, 167
"Three Wise Men," 111, 111*n.*
Trade Expansion Act, 163
Treaty of Cooperation, 12, 12*
Treaty of Rome, 61, 63*, 64, 66, 78, 81, 82, 83–84, 87, 99, 138.
Truman, Harry S., 126
Turkey, 88, 147
Tuthill, John W., 164

United States, 41, 55, 65, 102, 144
and Common Market, 157–159, 163–164, 168
farm exports, 163–165, 166
foreign aid, 36, 156
NATO, 33, 53, 125, 127–130
United States Atomic Energy Commission, 116–119

Verdun
Battle of, 11, 12, 14, 15, 25, 196
cemetery, 14*
city, 13–15, 17, 20
partition of (843), 21, 23

Washington, George, 161
West Germany, 15, 34, 44, 62, 86, 140
agriculture, 93–94, 96, 99, 100, 101, 104, 106–108
rearmament, 33–34, 53–54, 56
Western European Union (WEU), 56, 143, 145
Wilson, Harold, 155
workers, 80*, 81, 158*, 159*, 172, 173, 173*, 196
World Bank. *See* International Bank for Reconstruction and Development.
World War I, 11, 14–15, 25, 26
World War II, 13, 16, 26, 131

Photo Acknowledgments

The author and The World Publishing Company herewith render thanks to the Press and Information Services of the European Economic Community, Brussels, Belgium, for most of the illustrations used in *The Common Market*. Grateful acknowledgment is also made to the following:

Bredol-Lepper: Umschlag-Aussenseiten, for illustration on p. 20

French Embassy Press and Information Division, for illustrations on pp. 12, 14, and 124

German Information Center, for illustration on p. 18

New Zealand Consulate General, New York, for illustration on p. 149

Wide World Photos, Inc., for illustration on p. 160

About the Author

HARRY B. ELLIS gathered much of the material for his book on the Common Market during his recent assignment as the Paris Chief of Bureau for *The Christian Science Monitor*. Among the sources he drew upon were talks with Common Market and European leaders, including Jean Monnet, French Premier Georges Pompidou, and French Foreign Minister Couve de Murville, as well as his own travels and firsthand observations. Before this, Mr. Ellis was for many years a correspondent in the Middle East. He has written three books for adults: *Heritage of the Desert, Israel and the Middle East, Challenge in the Middle East*, and *The Arabs*, a Major Cultures book for children, published by World. In 1959 Mr. Ellis received the honorary degree of Doctor of Humane Letters from Wesleyan University in Middletown, Connecticut, for his writings on the Middle East.

Mr. Ellis is now staff correspondent for *The Christian Science Monitor* in Bonn, West Germany, where he lives with his family.

I 2 3 4 5 69 68 67 66 65